Spend and Grow Richer

—our old miser friend collected

Spend and Grow Richer

Do's and Don'ts of Investment

by Michael Malim

with illustrations by John Griffiths

J. M. Dent & Sons Limited London

For
Flavia,
Lydia,
Julia,
Delia
'all my pretty chickens and their dam',
Pam

First published 1972

Made in Great Britain
at the
Aldine Press · Letchworth · Herts
for
J. M. DENT & SONS LTD
Aldine House · Bedford Street · London

Hardback ISBN: 0 460 07884 4
Paperback ISBN: 0 460 02104 4

Contents

Pretext

'Daddy! Why do they have money if it doesn't keep its value? I mean, why have anything with value in it? Why not just let people swap things they don't want for things they do?'

My ten-year-old Delia—on hearing me blow my top about rising prices.

Me: 'Oh dear! What a question! To answer that I'd have to explain what money is—what value is . . .'

Delia: 'Oh, go on, please. Please tell me. I want to know.'

Me: 'Do you?'

Delia: 'Yes, I do.'

Me: 'Come to think of it, you ought to know. Everybody should. Far too few people do. If everybody did—if most people did—we'd hardly know ourselves. What money is—and isn't. What value is—and isn't. What investing is—and isn't. The way people get kidded and kid themselves—year after year, mainly because they don't understand the first things! Because they can't tell the difference. . . . Telling the difference, you know, is everything, really—whatever you're doing.'

Delia: 'Like marge from butter.'

Me: 'Like marge from butter, only more so.'

Delia: 'Tell me: please.'

Me: 'It'd take a young book.'

Delia: 'All right. You write it, then.'

Me: 'Thank you very much.'

Delia: 'Oh, please. . . .'

Some months later

Me: 'Here you are, then. . . . Read it through quickly first from beginning to end. Then go through it slowly bit by bit and test yourself with the questions to make sure you've understood.

'By the way, this is not—repeat not—a handbook on how to get rich quick (though you're unlikely to grow rich if you don't know what's in it). It's more of a handbook on how to avoid being wasteful—being a mug—being poor: on how to put and keep money in its proper place and *use* it well. If you know how to do that, you'll be much better equipped to do what's far more important—your own thing. You'll have the right attitude of mind.

'First of all, let me tell you a little story. . . .'

1 The Tool and the Job

1 Not long ago in a grandish country house, alone but for a handful of servants and hirelings of one kind or another, lived a rather dreary old miser. His father had left him some oil-wells in Texas and he owned a maze of companies, some of which shipped the crude oil from them here and there about the world, refined it and sold it in various forms through thousands of filling stations, while others ran hotels and banks and television stations, and heaven-knows-what-else. Consequently, he was stinking rich, as they say. At the same time he was as mean as only a very rich man can be. Some people reckoned he was the meanest man in the world, and it's quite on the cards they were right, though that is really neither here nor there. All that matters is that he was a miser and a fair old misery into the bargain, if not as a result.

Anyway, in this grandish country house of his lurked many treasures—marvellous paintings and other works of art, and many jewels—among them a huge diamond. To guard these treasures from thieves, the house was fitted with elaborate burglar alarms, detectives were always on duty in it, and fierce mastiffs roamed the grounds day and night—half starved to make and keep them as ferocious as possible.

Before the miser had acquired them, the pictures and other works of art had adorned the walls of palaces and great houses. Beautiful women had worn the jewels. The great diamond had dangled from the turbans of kings. In short, all the miser's treasures had been constantly on display, to impress people who saw them with the wealth and power of their owners.

Some of the people who saw them got great delight from their beauty but such people were fairly rare. The miser, poor soul, kept the works of art in a gallery under lock and key, the jewels in a strong-room under the ground. He had no eye or time either for company or beauty. He was far too busy day and night checking and measuring the value of all his different possessions. Getting richer and richer—that's to say owning more and more property and treasures—was his only interest—if you except his Skye terrier, MacTavish. His mother had been Scottish . . . and she and MacTavish were the only creatures that had ever loved him.

One day this miser died, and made headlines in newspapers all over the world because it's nice on the whole for people who lack wealth to hear about people who've had a vast amount of it. The huge collection of treasures he left was divided up among a number of people who had disliked him almost as much as he'd despised them. And since several of those who got works of art or jewels wanted other things instead, many of these treasures were sent to a famous firm of auctioneers in London to be sold, among them the great diamond.

The idea of an auction sale is to get lots of people who want something together into one room and tease them into bidding against each other so as to get as much for the thing as possible. This London firm is famous for auctioning rare treasures for very rich people all over the world, and when this sale took place the room was very full indeed of such people, including all the chief dealers in gems, paintings, sculptures and other works of art.

Among those who came from abroad (in his private aircraft) was a little, pot-bellied tycoon from Johannesburg. What he was after was that great diamond, not because he wanted to own it himself but because he had not long married a second wife, a beautiful woman young enough to be his daughter who was extremely clever at making him feel and look small in front of important people if he refused her anything. Unlike the miser, who had inherited his oil-wells, this tycoon was entirely self-made and, like most self-made men, what he wanted above all else was to look and feel big. So instead of hiding his treasures and possessions, he displayed them as much as possible—including the sleek second wife. The great diamond, she pointed out, would set her off a treat. He was getting it for her, she told everyone in his presence. How could he be anything like as big as he liked people to think if he failed to get it for her?

So he flew over to the sale, bought the thing after a great tussle for what you might call a king's ransom, and flew off with it pronto for home before he thought better of it, for, to tell the truth, he didn't much trust his sleek wife, and the thought of giving away to her so big a chunk of his hard earned fortune went a good deal against the grain. Suppose she left him. . . . Time and again he told himself in the plane he was being a fool. 'There's no fool like an old fool', he reflected. He kept eyeing the dark, handsome, tough young pilot. . . . There'd been whispers and hints that they had a fancy for each other. Once she had the diamond she would be rich. His own hold on her would be gone. Hell! If there was one thing he hated it was being diddled out of a possession.

While they were crossing Africa, something went wrong with the plane and they had to land in the back of beyond. The plane was damaged, but they got out more or less unhurt. The only thing they could do was to sit under a wing waiting for rescue. The pilot managed to radio their rough position. Help though was bound to take many days to arrive.

Days passed. Their water supply ran out. The only thing left to drink was beer, six cans of it in a carton which belonged to the pilot. There they sat under a wing of the bent plane, the tycoon with his diamond, the pilot with his six cans of beer. The radio had gone dead. . . . When the tycoon asked for a drink, the pilot remarked that if they shared the cans they'd both last, say, a week, whereas if one of them had all the beer he might last for a fortnight—perhaps more if he were young and strong.

Pretty soon, the tycoon was promising the pilot great rewards for half his beer—including the diamond. The pilot was certainly tempted but he knew the tycoon's promises and he shook his head. Moreover it struck him that there was no need, after all, for rescuers to find the tycoon alive. If it came to a showdown, the tycoon was old, small and flabby. His young wife would get much of his wealth. . . .

Much the same thoughts crossed the tycoon's mind at about the same time though in a different way. The pilot was still young but, he had often noticed, quick-tempered and impulsive if annoyed. Such people could be outwitted. He would have to be outwitted—rendered harmless—helpless—*dead?* Distinctly dead. By accident of course—to all intents and purposes. . . .

What would you say was the most valuable thing there under that wing? What, if anything, was worth a king's ransom?

Think carefully, now. The rest of this book will give you the answers—and the reasons.

2 Notice anything odd about that story? Nothing? Nothing, at any rate, in particular? All right, I'll tell you. *I never mentioned the word* '*money*'.

I used words like 'treasures'—'wealth'—'possessions'—'riches'—but not '*money*'.

I left it out on purpose as a matter of fact. The word I did make rather a point of using, however, was value. Value and valuable. This is the key word—value. All those other words, treasures and so on, imply or suggest value. They mean valuable things. But they don't necessarily imply or suggest money. At any rate, they shouldn't. Value and money are not the same thing.

This is the first thing you must well and truly get into your head. Money is not value. Value is not money. Say that over to yourself several times—now. And in bed before you drop off to sleep for a few nights: it'll stick. 'Money is not value. Value is not money.'

It's amazing—and very sad—how few people realize this: how few people can tell the difference, or keep from forgetting it.

Some people (according to television, anyway) can't tell marge from butter. It's a shame but not exactly serious. Others can't tell green from red—which can be dangerous at, say, crossroads. Most people can't tell a woodland mushroom from a meadow mushroom. Here, if you make a mistake, you may well not live to boast about it on the box or anywhere else.

Unless you're a born and incurable spendthrift (an interesting word, by the way, if you take it to pieces), not being able to tell money from value is unlikely to make you altogether dead, but it's pretty sure to make and keep you poor, which is generally speaking no way to live; though there are people who reckon it is and like it, but that's another story.

Can *you* tell money from value? You probably think you can, and *can*—up to a point. Up to what point, though? Not far enough probably. What *is* money? What *is* value? To be quite sure you'll always be able to spot the difference (a lot of people spend most of their time trying to pass the one off for the other—very artfully and very successfully) you really need to be quite sure what each of them is. So perhaps we'd better have a look at both.

Let's look first at money.

3 Money is a tool.

A tool is anything that can be used—anything that is or can be useful.

A thing is useful if it saves trouble, that's to say spares its user discomfort or gets him pleasure. If you find that difficult to believe, look at the things in your room. What is each thing there for? A chair saves people the discomfort of standing. A picture decorates—that is to say it's pleasant to look at. So are flowers in a bowl.

Pretty well anything you can think of can be useful to somebody some time for some purpose or other: can be, that's to say, a tool.

Chairs, sofas and couches are resting tools. Pictures and flowers are decorating tools, vases and bowls are containing tools *and*, usually, decorating tools.

Most things have a main use and can be put to other uses by the way, but few if any things can be of any use at all except to *some* people *some*where at *some* time. Not to all, everywhere, always. The great diamond our tycoon friend had bought for a king's ransom in London was useless on the face of it to him or anyone else under that aircraft wing 'somewhere' in Africa.

Money is a unique kind of tool. First of all, it's a swapping tool. To be useful as a swapping tool, it has to measure value: so it's also a measuring tool. To measure value it has to contain it, so it's also a containing tool.

There are other tools which contain as well as measure. A milk bottle, for instance, contains a pint usually of milk; a carton of sugar half a pound, say, of sugar. The bottle or carton can be useful for containing something else. The bottle can measure other liquids.

Money, though, is useless unless it contains value, and it can only measure value. To measure value properly then, any 'piece' of money—a 50p piece, say—should always contain the same amount of value.

A tape measure to be useful must contain so much length, so many inches, feet, yards. If it stretches or shrinks, it won't measure properly. If a milk bottle were elastic (like a balloon, say), you'd never know how much milk you were getting.

That's just the snag about money. It *is* elastic. What's worse, as far as one can see, it's bound to be, nowadays.

4 Long, long ago when the Carthaginians went trading with the Mauretanians of West Africa, they used to heave-to their ships off the coast, row ashore, spread their goods along the beach, then return to their ships and wait. After a while, the Mauretanians would emerge, spread *their* offerings along the beach and retire. If the Carthaginians didn't think the

Mauretanians were offering enough, they'd sit tight till the Mauretanians put up more. Similarly, the Mauretanians lay low if they reckoned the Carthaginians were being mean. There'd be to-ing and fro-ing. Eventually, when both sides were happy, they met, swapped and went their ways. You can bet your bottom dollar, by the way, that the Carthaginians got the better of the bargain more often than not. They were very artful at trade. What's more, they must have had money at home and used it when they traded elsewhere, or they couldn't possibly have become as civilized as they did. The Mauretanians clearly didn't have money of their own, and saw no use for anyone else's—at any rate not the Carthaginian kind. So they had to go in for this way of trading called 'barter'. Bartering still goes on in some parts of the world among primitive people—up the Amazon, for instance. And governments barter a great deal, but we needn't bother about that just now.

The snag about barter, of course, is that it's so terribly clumsy. In a very, very simple village community, the butcher, the baker, the farmer, the cobbler, the carpenter, the doctor, the lawyer, old Uncle Tom Cobbleigh and all can make do after a fashion by swapping their goods and know-how. Even so, just imagine the arguments over 'I want this or that' and 'How much of your rubbish is worth how much of my treasures'. Obviously no community which lived by barter could ever be anything but very simple. Society as we know it would be impossible without money. What could *you* offer to your Gas or Electricity Boards, or to British Rail, say, or to your local shops for what you want from them—that they would accept? And what would you regard in the way of *things* as fair pay for your work—that your employer would want to pass on to you?

Gradually barterers took to giving and taking tokens—things of a kind pretty well everyone wanted anywhere at any time because everyone thought them always useful and thereby attached a value to them. Things, though, that weren't just anybody's for the taking such as, say, sticks and stones.

Weird and wonderful things have done duty as money at different times in different parts of the world. Feathers, for instance, stones, cowrie-shells, *human skulls*, cattle—even elephants (for big deals, presumably). But why on earth, you may ask, should *everyone* want feathers, stones, shells—or human skulls? What *use* would they be? Surely stones, shells

What could you offer to . . . British Rail, say . . . ?

and feathers at least are easy enough to come by? True; but these surely were special feathers, stones, shells and skulls. They were ones that contained or possessed something everyone could use—magical powers. At any rate, everybody thought they did because Powerful People said they did. And you needn't smile at them for that either, because people aren't very much less gullible about money today, even though it is not exactly magical powers they value it for. But most financiers like to be thought of as 'wizards': it pays. They aren't, though. They're simply in the know.

Still, these things were pretty clumsy apart from other drawbacks; the traders, pedlars especially, must have been always on the look-out for something handier and more reliable everybody would use every day.

The ancient Ethiopians used salt. Everybody could do with salt—all the time. You could weigh it out in different standard amounts. Salt was recognizably salt. It didn't go bad, at any rate, not quickly. And you could lug it around without too much trouble.

And there you glimpse the five things money must be to do a good job—to be a good swapping tool. Firstly, it must be something everybody could do with at any time, anywhere. Secondly, it must be something you can weigh out or measure out exactly. Thirdly, it must be something of more or less fixed quality. Fourthly, it must be something which doesn't rot or dwindle, at any rate, at all quickly. Fifthly, it must be something which can be easily carried about and stored.

Salt wasn't bad. It kept its saltiness—i.e. usefulness—well enough, and one bag of salt was much like another. Presumably it was in hard lumps—rock salt. It could be weighed out. But if it was easier to cart about and store than skulls, stones or what-have-you, it wasn't all that handy.

I mentioned 'weighing it out'. How much was so much? The Ethiopians presumably had standard—that's to say 'official'—weights and measures. Without them, obviously, every swap of this or that would involve bargaining—*enough* salt of such or such a kind or quality. . . . Bartering, in fact, of a sort, and still pretty clumsy. . . . But how much was *enough*?

What one badly needed, obviously, were tokens which, everyone could take it for granted, contained a definite amount of a definite quality—of something: *standard* tokens, official. Vouched for by Authority.

Metals were the obvious things to make them of. They could be 'minted' in handy sizes. They weren't too easy to come by. They didn't go bad or evaporate. Metal could be 'assayed' for quality, and tokens of it stamped by Authority, and so guaranteed to contain so much metal of such and such a quality. They could be made difficult to counterfeit, and Authority could make life hell for anyone caught counterfeiting.

Some metals corrode more quickly than others. Gold doesn't corrode at all, silver very slowly, copper less quickly than most. Each could be precisely refined and assayed. There was a fair amount of each in the ground here and there, but not enough to make them common or easy to get hold of. These then were the ideal metals for the job—to make handy, reliable tools for swapping.

Even so, there was still one very considerable drawback.

5 So coins—official tokens made of precious metal—must have gradually come into being all over the world: tokens that everyone would accept as standard measures of value *because they took it for granted everyone else would.* Even so, as I said, there was a drawback. For traders making big deals far from home, coins were, in bulk, very heavy and clumsy to hump around; and they made ideal loot for bandits, highwaymen, footpads, cutpurses, pirates, pick-pockets, burglars, thieves, robbers and any other villains with an eye for the main chance if only because nobody could ever prove this or that coin or collection of them properly belonged to *him* and had been pinched from *him*. There was no telling one 'piece of eight' from any other.

Anyway, traders took to giving I O Us to people who would take them, these being written promises to pay (in coin) known as promissory or pro-notes.

Obviously, no one would take an IOU or pro-note except from someone he could trust or unless it was guaranteed by someone he could trust. Moreover there wouldn't be much sense in taking a pro-note from anyone from far away if you had to go there and collect the coins yourself. So banks came into being as local guardians and stockists of coins that local traders could take pro-notes to—and get payment for—in coins. What these bankers were doing was buying pro-notes for money, hoping to sell them to other people at a profit or aiming to present them direct in due course to the traders who originally issued them. To make their profit, they'd pay a bit less in coin for each pro-note than its face value, i. e. 'charge a discount'. Pro-notes of course were tokens themselves of a kind—private tokens—and how much in the way of coins (official money) bankers would give for any particular pro-note depended on how far they reckoned the original issuer could be trusted to keep his promise by paying up in official coins himself—how rich and honest, in other words, he was known to be. If no one locally had ever heard of him, his pro-notes would be worthless locally unless he persuaded or conned people into trusting him. If he was very well known locally to be rich and honest, on the other hand, his pro-notes could be 'as good as gold'. Hence the expression.

Many different kinds of private tokens have gradually come into use under various names such as bills, drafts, 'kites', bonds, money-orders, certificates, warrants, coupons, 'negotiable instruments' and so on. They're all either IOUs or orders-to-pay: and though many of them are useless to what you might call the 'manual villains' on the whole, they do offer golden opportunities to the white-collar varieties such as forgers, fakers, embezzlers, cheats, swindlers, pushers, artful charlies and con-men in general whose job in life is to relieve you, me and the next him or her of value without our noticing it—at any rate for the time being.

Which brings us to value. . . .

But what I wanted to say before going on to that is that this is how *paper* money came into being—with bank-notes and currency notes. First traders then bankers took to issuing their own pro-notes, for the convenience of themselves and their customers. Eventually, Authority, i. e. governments, took to doing so instead of 'minting' actual tokens of precious metal as standard units of value. This they took to doing first because they were short of the metals, later for other reasons. Look at any currency note and you'll see it says 'I promise to pay . . .' Pay what?

That, as the politicians say, is a good question.

Nowadays the answer is—nothing: at any rate the promise won't—and can't—be kept in *precious* metals.

Well, what's a currency note worth, then? It's a fair question: more than fair: crucial. The key question, really.

For one thing, what's happened is that all money nowadays has become, for practical purposes, 'credit'. Even coins are no longer what they were. In the old days if you melted a coin down you had so much gold, silver or copper which pretty well anyone would gladly accept after weighing and assaying. Try melting down any modern coin and seeing what anyone will give you for the resulting blob of 'alloy'!

Credit means trustworthiness.

6 'A horse! A horse! My kingdom for a horse!' gasped Richard III fleeing from Bosworth Field, according to Shakespeare, anyway. In the same way, our tycoon friend might have whimpered 'My diamond (or my fortune) for three of those cans of beer'! Not that many people who heard Richard would have wanted his kingdom. Probably many of those who had horses would have preferred—that's to say 'put a higher value on'—their horses to any kingdom. Kingdoms aren't by any means everyone's cup of tea; nor horses, for that matter.

In any case, nobody with any gumption would have taken Richard's offer. They'd have reckoned that he no longer had a kingdom to swap. In other words, he had no 'credit' left; precious little anyway.

Value, in short, is something somebody 'puts on something'—'attaches' to it. It measures how much he wants to get it or keep it. In other words, it's really a feeling in the first place. 'I attach a lot of value to this or that,' people say. As often as not, if you ask 'How much?' there's no answer, or something vague. 'I'd give my eyes for it' or 'I'd rather die than part with it'. Eyes or life are *prices* which are *personal* measures of value—what somebody will give or take to keep or acquire something. *Personal* measures. No two people often, if ever, attach the same value to anything. One *wants* it more than the other. When it comes to *price*, some people can *afford* to give more than others.

A thing has value because people want it, and people want it because it could be useful to them: and a thing can be useful simply because it has value. Value is useful because it's a tool for getting other tools with. The more value—not things—you own, the richer you are. So the things rich people want are the things with the most value in them. The rich put it there.

That, you may say, goes without saying. The point is though that people often say 'value' when they mean 'price', and it's important to realize which they really do mean, especially when they're at all likely to be artful charlies. The poorest man in the world can set as much *value* on a thing as a

Value, in short, is something somebody 'puts' on something

millionaire but he can't pay anything like the *price* the millionaire can.

It's because people are careless about which word they use that there seem to be different kinds of value—e.g. market value, sentimental value and intrinsic value. Market value isn't value; it's price—the price something should fetch in a market. Intrinsic value is merit—what something deserves to be worth but isn't because too few people realize how useful (or useless) it could be and most, as a result, under- or overrate it. Sentimental value is the value someone attaches to something he has because *he* wants it around, gets pleasure from seeing it and fears he'd miss it if he lacked it. . . in short it's just value. Every tool, remember, either gives pleasure or relieves discomfort, and there are many kinds and degrees of either. But some things can only do their job for one or two particular people. Kidney machines, for instance.

Of course it's value that makes bargains, but it's the value attached by two or more people, not just one. Other people may attach little or no value to something you treasure, so it'll fetch a small price if offered for sale unless you offer it to somebody who wants it as much as you do, possibly for quite a different reason.

At Bosworth Field, Richard III priced his kingdom at a horse: our tycoon marooned in Africa priced his great diamond at three cans of beer. These are barter prices, of course. In the ordinary way, prices are set in terms of money. And things priced in this way are commonly said to be 'valued'. Not that valuation has to be done in terms of money. 'Worth a king's ransom,' one says, or 'Not worth a row of beans.' But money terms are convenient.

They can also be very misleading.

You see, as I said some while back, money is a tool like anything else that is usable. It's only useful if it contains so much value itself, put on it or attached to it by *everybody*. Everybody will only attach so much value to it if everybody assumes that everybody else will do the same.

When money was gold, silver or copper, everyone could take the value of a coin for granted—more or less. (Authority though was always apt to fiddle the amount or quality of precious metals in coins—debase them, as they say.)

The job of money is to contain value and hold it—a regular amount of it. The snag nowadays is—it doesn't hold it. It's a rotten container. It leaks—like nobody's business.

Which is fine for some people, especially the artful charlies, but a lot less than fine for simpletons: not to mention mugs, who are, as you know, born at the rate of one a minute, and are around, as a result, in very great numbers.

7 Well-off people have lots of money. Do they? Very seldom actually. They mostly *use* a lot of money—that's to say, spend it—but that's quite a different thing. People who motor use a great deal of petrol, but they don't often *have* a lot of it. They just buy a few gallons at a time, as and when they need it.

What well-off people have is means—that's to say property of one kind or another. When they need money, they hire it, as a rule. If you have means, it's pretty easy to hire money: if you haven't, it's very difficult. (Banks and so on talk of 'borrowing' and 'lending' money when they mean 'hiring'.) When you borrow or lend something, you don't pay or charge anything, and the idea is that you give or get the actual thing back again. When you hire or let something, you pay or make a charge for so much use of it. The charge for hiring money is called 'interest'. This is *very* important to understand; when you buy something on hire purchase what you hire is the money to pay for the thing, and the charge (interest) is, nine times out of ten, miles stiffer than you imagine—if you do imagine, which most people don't, not knowing what they're actually doing, and having been carefully lulled. But that's by the way for the moment.

The thing is, these well-off people who hire money when they need it are using money properly—simply for spending. That's all money is for. Money is for spending, and don't let anyone kid you into thinking it has any other use whatever.

Value is another matter. Value is for getting.

Money is for spending. Value is for getting, keeping, collecting.

Well-off people are *worth* a lot of money, yes. What they *have* is a lot of value—stored, as it were, in property of one kind or another. If all their property were sold, i.e. 'swapped' for money, it would fetch a lot of money.

Money, you see, is merely *a* kind of property.

Property is another of those words which is apt to be misleading because people use it or take it to mean different things. Mostly, it's used to mean land and buildings. But in reality, anything that's owned is a property.

This means that any tool is a property, because anything

that's usable is a tool, and anything that's usable is wanted and more or less sure to be owned by somebody or other. Money is a tool, so money is a kind of property.

Any tool—any property—contains value, a different amount of it for each person who wants the thing. Those who want it a lot will attach more value to it than those who want it less: and those who don't want it at all will attach no value to it at all. The price any 'wanter' will pay to get it from its owner will depend partly on how much value he attaches to it and partly on how much value he can afford to give—whether in money or in something else. Value is the point. When you buy or sell something (whether using money or bartering), you swap *value* in something for *value* in something else—whether you mean to or not.

Whose value? That's the question. Yours or somebody else's?

Suppose you sold, shall we say, your sewing-machine which you don't use to somebody for his mowing-machine which he doesn't use. You don't attach much value to your sewing-machine and he doesn't attach much to his mowing-machine. So the value you swap is not much unless, of course, either your sewing-machine or his mowing-machine is much more valuable in some way than you or he thought. What you were both after was the *usefulness* of the other's machine to sew or mow with, not the *value* it might have for somebody else altogether.

Suppose though your sewing-machine wouldn't work at all but was the first one ever made. It would be useless to sew with, so the other chap could only want it for its *value* to someone else—as a 'collector's piece'—a curio—an antique. People collect such rarities for various reasons, but more often than not because they think others will want them more and more and so attach more and more value to them.

When you buy anything for its value, not for the use it was made for, you *invest* in it. Getting possession of it is *investment*. Anything owned for the sake of its *value* is an investment.

The 'means' that well-off people have lots of are investments—properties usually of many different kinds bought for the sake of the value to be stored in them and got out of them, one way or another. Usually such people hold a good many different kinds of property because they know that any kind or piece of property is as apt to lose value as gain it as time goes by, even very suddenly (with the possible exception of precious stones). And since wealth is simply a lot of value, you need a fair mixture of different sorts of properties to keep your stock of value in, as it were, so that value lost by some can be made up with value gained by others.

The kind of property shrewd, well-off people will never hold much of, though—at any rate for long—is money, because they know that money loses value more or less all the time; is pretty well bound to, things being the way they are, for the time being at all events: and is highly unlikely ever to *gain* value.

8 Our old miser friend had a vast amount of value stored in masses of different properties. So had the tycoon, if a good deal less. Both had spent much of their lives collecting value and done precious little else: the miser really nothing else. Alone and palely loitering among his treasures, the miser seemed a pretty miserable creature, but presumably it was the life he wanted. The little tycoon liked strutting about and showing off, being much afraid of people looking down on him. If he were rich, he hoped, people would admire him, or at least pretend to. The young pilot, on the other hand, wanted to live and have exciting adventures of one sort or another. Under that aircraft wing, he had visions of the adventurous life he could lead, with the help of the value in that diamond. Going on expeditions to legendary places and becoming a famous explorer, or, at any rate, adventurer. How wasted, he thought, all that value was on 'Old Blubberguts' or his greedy little wife, for that matter! What a chance to be shot of him—and her: of everyone: to be at nobody's beck and call: to be his own master: to be free!

Had he accepted the offer of the diamond for three of his cans of beer, the pilot would have been *investing* his own value in the beer in opulent appetite—in Jo'burg or somewhere—for the diamond. Plainly, it would be a risky investment: he'd halve his chance of survival, and he knew that the tycoon could never be trusted to keep his word if he could gain by breaking it, which was one reason why he was so rich. It would be so easy later on, if they were rescued, for the tycoon to convince people that he had been robbed.

The tycoon, on the other hand, would not have been *investing*: he wanted the beer to relieve thirst—one of the jobs it was made for—not for the sake of its value to anyone somewhere else, which would obviously be trivial. Or would he? I'm asking *you.*

I mention all this partly to show what an investment is—getting and collecting value—and partly to show what widely different reasons people have for investing. Misers collect value simply for the pleasure or comfort of having it: tycoons usually for the pleasure of showing off or for the relief of the discomfort of feeling small. Others, like the pilot, for the pleasure of being free to live their own lives their own way and escape from the discomforts of being employed—that's to say, 'used' by other people: in other words, for the joys of independence.

These are extreme cases of course. Most people invest without any clearer aim than having something 'put by for a rainy day' or 'a spot of comfort when they retire'. They feel they ought to 'save a bit' and 'not have their money idle'. That's all right as far as it goes, but it's a very short way. Some of them don't do so badly. A lot do, though. They miss a great deal, and plenty of them actually lose, because they don't realize that *value* is leaking out of their investments—at any rate until it's too late to do anything much about it. Not that it's ever too late to set about recovering value lost, but the particular pleasures or reliefs you need the value to buy may already have slipped beyond your reach.

Getting, collecting and keeping value—investing, that is to say—is an art or job that is better done methodically than casually. The first thing you must do to do anything methodically is to decide as precisely as possible what you want to do it for: have an aim—a target (or several). A target is something so big so far away. As far as investing is concerned, this means collecting enough value to buy certain 'tools' you can get pleasure or relief of discomfort with in so many weeks', months' or years' time.

And here's a curious thing about investment targets. The bigger and nearer an ordinary target is, the easier it is to hit. With investment targets, it's exactly the opposite: it's far more difficult to hit a big target in a short while than a small one in several years' time. This is why gambling is so popular. There are only three ways of making a 'fortune overnight': theft—marriage—and gambling. The first two can cost you dear. The third means trusting to luck. Gambling is *not* investing: you want to be quite clear about this, if only because the artful charlies take endless pains to persuade people that it is.

Bookies, for instance. If you fall for it, *you* gamble, *they* invest.

In either case, of course, you can gain value or lose it. When you invest, however, you are (or should be) *likelier* to gain it than lose it. When you gamble, you are *likelier* to lose it than gain it. How much likelier depends. It's often very difficult to know whether a possible deal is a gamble or an investment. If it's investment you're after, however, regard it when in doubt as a gamble.

There's always *some* risk, you see, in investment, and if it's a target you're after, there's no point in taking any more risk than you need.

Targets. . . .

In the good old days (which were good for a few people and more or less horrible for most), if you owned no value—were 'worthless'—you became destitute. Skill is, of course, a 'tool', or 'property', so anyone with a 'skill' has value for anyone who wants to use it: the difficulty may be to find anyone who does. More people may possess the skill than its 'wanters' need: if so, the value of the skill is bound to be low and it'll fetch little or nothing in the way of a wage—that's to say price or charge—if offered for hire. All too many people used to have, for practical purposes, no skill at all. The only 'tools' or 'properties' they possessed were their eyes, ears, noses, tongues, arms, legs, hands and muscles in general—plus their wits; and the only jobs they could be used for were, therefore, 'menial'—to push, pull, lift, fetch and carry and so on—like animals: as 'labourers', in fact; jobs any 'able-bodied' person could do, so of very small value. The hire price they could get when they were wanted was barely enough 'to keep body and soul together'. The moment they weren't wanted, 'destitution stared them in the face'. Life was a 'hand to mouth' affair—and destitution spelled starvation. Dread of it certainly was very great for most people, though the well-off certainly dreaded it most.

In those days well-off people used badly-off people (except when they were slaves) much more heartlessly, as a rule, than they used their cattle, simply because they owned no value in them: they were very useful for drudgery, and could be replaced at no cost if broken or worn out. Slaves, like cattle, were an investment as well as useful as labouring 'tools', so it paid to take care of them.

Earning a decent living a hundred years ago—or even less—was a far chancier business than nowadays. You could fall out of your niche at any time, and if you did your chances of climbing into another were slim indeed. Destitution stalked all but the really rich all the time. A goodly stock of value—in properties—which could make you independent was therefore highly desirable. The safest and soundest kind of property to invest in was good land and buildings, especially farmland: everyone needed home-grown food.

So, once you'd 'made your pile' you invested in a country estate (or several), bought or built yourself a stately home and a town house, and lived graciously off the rents you charged farmers, labourers and other tenants for using your land, farmsteads, villages and cottages. In other words, you drew value from other people, which they paid you for the right to use bits of yours.

The snag about this system was that most of the value got into the hands of very few people, and most people had little or none and couldn't get it either, because the more you had the easier it was to get more; and nobody much likes parting with what he has if he can help it, least of all the very rich. If there's one thing most rich people can't bear, it's the thought of any of their property getting into the hands of somebody they don't know or aren't related to.

In those days, and till quite recently, really, you were free to collect and keep as much value as you could lay your hands on and pocket anything you could get from hiring out your properties. Nowadays, though, the Government keeps common stocks of value for dishing out to people who have little or none of their own, to save them from becoming destitute. This stock it gets almost entirely from taxation, that's to say by making people and businesses hand over chunks of the new value they get possession of every year through toiling, trading or hiring out their properties. At the same time, people with only common skills to hire out have been able, by banding together in unions, to push up their hire charges or wages. . . . As a result, far fewer people have to live 'from hand to mouth' or in dread of destitution, and though the very rich can still quite easily stay very rich, living in stately homes and town or country seats is no longer so gracious because you can't get enough domestics to wait on you hand and foot in them for love or money these days. Being used (employed) is not every man's idea of fun but it is a lot less humiliating than being a utensil—even a treasured one.

Grandees—the nobility, the gentry, squires—all had one

thing in common. They were all *rentiers*, as the French called them: people who lived (very nicely, as a rule) on regular cuts of other people's value. Their ancestors (for the most part) had invested in *rights*: rights and titles, properties, that's to say, which 'entitled' them to 'enjoy' certain 'powers'. All properties, if you look at them closely, are rights to use or enjoy something and often, though not always, deny its use to other people. Without your leave, no one has a right to use your car; a bus or rail ticket entitles you to be carried by bus or train from here to there, but not to stop others from travelling with you.

Nationalization of this or that simply cuts down the number of 'rights' you can invest in to levy a cut on the value of other people. Social security, on the other hand, bestows 'rights' to a cut or cuts of the common stock of value which is fed by taxation of one kind or another.

Rights. Rights are 'properties' licensed by the Law. There is nothing sacred about them, though the way some people talk about them they seem to think so. Laws are for obeying—and changing.

Rights provide means. Without means, you must take what you're given and do what you're told. Investing buys means. Means give you some independence—some freedom. How much do you want? Nobody nowadays can get the amount or kind of licensed freedom the old-time grandees enjoyed. You can still get an enormous amount of it, though, through investment if you know what you're doing—and do it! Or enough. You don't have to aim at being a tycoon or a miser, but it's as well to have some 'private means'.

9 Point one, then. Investing is spending. It's not saving. You can spend without investing, but you can't invest without spending.

Money is *for* spending: it has no other use. It's a property or 'tool' for swapping. You can spend it on—swap it for—things for their usefulness or for their value. If you spend it on things for their value, you invest in them.

Right?

To have something to spend (not necessarily money) on value, you plainly mustn't keep spending your all on 'commodities'—which means things which afford comfort, pleasure or convenience but lose value through use. Saving is *not* spending on commodities. If you don't spend what you save though, you're merely hoarding, which won't get you anywhere if what you're hoarding is losing value or, at least, not gaining any. You must spend it pronto on some property which will (with luck) get you more value sooner or later than you pay to get hold of it.

'Not necessarily money,' I said. People talk about 'putting a lot of work—effort—energy—skill—trouble—time—into a job, task, undertaking or venture'. Skill, energy and time are all properties or 'tools' containing value which are useful for getting—and keeping—value. Our old miser had inherited a great deal of value and spent all his time, skill and energy keeping it and amassing more.

Our tycoon, on the other hand, had set out with practically nothing but his (and his wife's) wits, skill and energy to invest, and had spent pretty well all he had ever since on amassing value, making his fortune. The pilot, however, spent almost all the energy, skill and time he had left after earning his pay on fun-and-games—not to mention most of his pay plus money he'd borrowed from other people.

Mind you, he'd put a lot of energy and time into becoming a skilful pilot in the past, and his salary was the return for this investment from which he got his fun-and-games. Not that he was content, as you know. He was really unwilling though to spend less time, energy and money on fun-and-games in order to spend the saving on getting the skill to get more value with, but this was partly because he took it for granted that he had no 'head for figures' and wouldn't succeed if he tried. Vast numbers of people have the same idea and don't try, either, which is a very good thing for the financiers and a very good thing indeed for the artful charlies, simpletons being the ideal customers for the former and mugs for the latter. Simpletons and mugs are people who can't tell whether a proposition is good, bad or indifferent because they don't know what to look for (apart from being much too ready to take things on trust). They think—usually because they've been taught to—that finance and investment are mysteries only very clever people can hope to understand, which is, believe me, nonsense. You don't have to be an expert to invest tolerably well, any more than you have to be Yehudi Menuhin to play the fiddle nicely or Tony Jacklin to put up a decent show at golf. What you must have is a proper grasp of certain principles, an eye for conditions, some knowledge of what's what, and gumption about seeking, choosing and taking expert advice.

It's the same with anything else. Nobody can know everything about anything, much less about everything.

Point two, then. Unless you're born with a silver spoon in your mouth, as they used to say, the only assets, i.e. properties, i.e. 'tools', you start off with are your wits, senses or faculties, limbs, organs and muscles—plus energy. Energy's the key tool of doing, just as value's the key tool of getting. With value at your disposal, you can get the properties, mostly rights of one kind or another, which you can get more value with. At birth, your energy's worth everything to you to bawl with for attention. But it's worth nothing to anyone else.

As you know, however, you can use energy, that's to say, 'invest' it, in developing skill for your wits, faculties, limbs, organs, etc., which has value for others. Since most people like doing what they're best at, the best investment for any boy or girl is, obviously, in his or her own talents, gifts, aptitudes. Merely by going to school or college you invest in skills up to a point. But the skills they teach you are taught to crowds of others, so they can't have much 'market value'. It's the rare property, in the right place at the right time, which attracts most of that. Rarity is something only you can apply to your own skill or gift. What makes anything rare is what's different about it, what's original. If you can get publicity for your difference or originality, you can attract fans, audiences, spectators, readers, viewers, listeners, clients. People who can attract a following—authors, entertainers, athletes, artists, doctors, advocates—and so collect value in themselves can be the freest of all. *Can* be, as long as they insist on using themselves and not being used by other people. Unfortunately some skills and talents fade, fashions change, and publishers have to follow fashion to stay in business. Few assets have less value than dead fame.

Which is why wise 'soloists' who depend much on youth, health or fashion for their success invest much of their value elsewhere while it's high: while the going is good.

While their skills are in good demand. . . .

While people will pay good money to see, hear, watch, consult or hire them; or buy their works.

Demand makes Value. Value makes Market. Market makes Price. And Price, as a rule, spells . . . M O N E Y.

1 Test Yourself Questions

You should know the answers at once.
If in doubt, read the indicated sections carefully again.

1 Money is a tool. What is its main job? What other jobs must it do to do its main job properly? What is its main weakness now? [Section 3]

2 What are the five things money must be to be 'good' money? What is missing with modern money? [Section 4]

3 Why did substitutes for coins come into use? What are the two kinds of substitutes? [Section 5]

4 What is credit? [Section 5]

5 What is value? What is price? Is value a tool? If so, what is it useful for? [Section 6]

6 What is investing? What is the point of it? What is the difference between investing and gambling? [Sections 7 and 9]

7 What is a property? What are means? What are rights? [Sections 7 and 9]

2 Holding Your Own

1 By now, I hope, you can tell value from money. The next thing you must be able to do is recognize money when you see it. It comes and goes, you see, in many shapes, forms and guises, not to mention disguises. Originally there were those skulls, shells, feathers, salt and so on. Next coins, then IOUs or pro-notes and money-orders, private and official. Nowadays official money—currency—'cash in circulation', as they say, the stuff you can take into any shop in the country and swap for this or that, consists of 'bank-notes' and metal tokens. Actually they're both mere tokens.

Mere tokens. That is to say, they merely *stand for* money.

Real money—the money that matters—is credit.

Credit, as you know, is trustworthiness.

It all goes back to this business of IOUs, etc. 'So-and-so,' you hear people say, has 'plenty of money in the bank.' This doesn't mean he has bags and boxes of notes and coins—official tokens—in there labelled Mr So-and-so. It means that the bank has a large number of pounds 'entered' in a book (or on a tape) to his name—*credited* to him. It means that if he tells his bank to pay money for him to someone else, the bank will do so. Why? Because it owes him money which he's already put into it—the amount *credited* to his 'account' in that book.

How did he put the money in? He might have paid in official tokens. Much more likely he'd paid in cheques or other kinds of money-order. A cheque is simply a kind of letter telling a bank to pay money for somebody to somebody else. Postal-orders are likewise 'letters' telling the Post Office to hand over money to whoever 'demands' it. There are lots of other kinds of money-orders which call on somebody or some business or other to pay out money 'on demand'—when the letter is 'presented'.

Far more money, probably, changes hands in the form of 'money-orders' every day of the week than in 'cash'—i.e. official tokens.

A money-order is not the same thing as an IOU or pro-note. A pro-note says 'I promise to pay' so much money, whether 'on demand', that is to say whenever the note is

So much money on demand

'presented' to 'me', or on some future date. A money-order says 'Pay on my behalf'.

In the one case 'I' might break 'my' promise. In the other, whoever is told to pay may refuse to do so. This is where the trustworthiness or credit comes in. If the person who 'issues' the IOU is thought likely to pay, then his IOU is good; if not, it's bad. Likewise, a money-order is good if the person or business ordered to pay is thought to be able—and likely to be willing—to pay the amount; and bad if he or it isn't.

IOUs and money-orders are 'messages' on bits of paper which bestow 'rights'—rights to get dues out of somebody or some business. Dues are usually—but not always—money.

Rights are properties.

Properties contain value.

Any property that's likely to net you sooner or later, if you get hold of it, more value than you pay for it, is an investment. So, if you can buy somebody else's IOU or money-order and get more *value* out of it than you give for it, you've made a sound investment in it. Buying other people's dues or debts, in other words, can be a profitable thing to do.

So. When you invest, you *buy* a right which may enable you to draw *value* from some kind of property or other. Your right or bunch of rights, written on paper, is commonly known as a 'security'. It 'secures' your rights in Law. It's 'acceptable' evidence in a Court of Law.

Most 'securities' prove rights to draw *money* from some 'concern' or other—whether it be Government, a company, a society or a particular person. *Money*. Not value.

Money loses value. Investing in money, then—money in any form—is apt to be unwise, because the whole object of investing is to *gain* value—not *lose* it.

'Apt to be,' I said, and 'money in any form.' Thanks to 'loopholes', really rich people like our miser and tycoon can do very nicely indeed by investing in money in certain ways. Never mind them though. You and I seldom can. What's more, we're so easily gulled or conned, as the artful charlies know only too well, through being unable to recognize money in disguise. As a result, *we* tend to get the money, while *they* get the value. As ever, it's the make-up—the fancy packaging they take us in with. Artful's not the word for it.

You can learn to see through it though. With a bit of trouble, it's not all that difficult. Then you must keep your eyes skinned. . . .

2 The trouble is there are no reliable measures of value like feet and inches of length, pints and quarts of liquid, ounces, pounds, stones, etc., of weight. Money's supposed to do the job, but doesn't and probably can't. Remember that tape measure which shrinks all the time—sometimes fast, sometimes slowly; and can occasionally stretch a little! That's what money's like as a measure of value.

Let's invent a standard measure to show what happens. Let's call it a Val. A pound note always contains, shall we say, 100 Vals *when you get it*. Money, let's assume, is going to lose value at an *average* rate of 5 per cent of its content a year for several years. You put your note, when you get it, into a money-box and leave it there. A year later, you'll still have a pound but probably only 95 Vals. After five years you'll probably have only 76.5 Vals. After ten, only 59 Vals. And so on.

Suppose you took a job at a salary of £2,000 a year; it will get you 200,000 Vals. That's what you think! If your salary is paid at the end of each month, you'll get fewer and fewer Vals each month. If you don't get rises, your salary will really be going down and down each year, and even if you do, it'll still be going down not up if they're not large enough. In *value*, that is, of course.

What you'll have done is to invest your own value pretty badly. Your employer, on the other hand, will have invested his well in your skill—if you do your job well: strictly speaking, to keep even with him, you should obviously give him proportionately *less* skill every montn! But there's no reliable measure of that either, unfortunately.

Suppose now you put ten pounds, say, into some 'Savings Scheme' which promises to pay you 5 per cent a year. You'll have invested your tenner in—that's to say *spent* it on—the right to draw fifty pence in interest a year from the scheme, and on presentation of the certificate—the security—to be paid ten pounds (your capital) 'on demand'. So at the end of the year you have the right to £10.50. Money is losing value at, say, 5 per cent a year—5 Vals in each pound. Your ten pounds originally contained 1,000 Vals. After a year, ten pounds contain only 950 Vals: but you'll have gained fifty pence. These though contain only 47.5 of *last year*'s Vals, so you'll have 997.5 'old' Vals altogether—2.5 less than you invested. Suppose though you have to pay income tax on that 'interest' of 5 per cent, then you'll have still fewer of the old Vals than you invested. This would have been better than keeping the ten pounds for a year in a money-box which would have lost you 50 Vals—a lot more—but it would still have been a bad investment. You'd have more money, true, but less value.

Since it's more value you're after, you must obviously do some careful arithmetic before you put any of your money into any 'Savings Scheme' which offers you a 'fixed rate of interest' and won't pay you your money back on demand or at very short notice. Otherwise you risk ending up with less value than you started with—a lot less. It's terrifying, really, how many people who invested in money one way and another years ago are regretting it bitterly now. Many of them have become very poor indeed.

3 If there was one thing 'Old Blubberguts' knew backwards it was how to use this 'tool', money, to collect value with. He had learnt the ropes in childhood and youth, haggling and peddling for dear life about the backyards and alleys of a city in Central Europe. This was back in the twenties when money actually became valueless in many countries of Europe, though not in Britain, which was enormously rich, holding a vast collection of rights all over the world inside and outside her Empire.

Terrible poverty led to Fascism in Italy and Nazism in Germany in the thirties. A year or so before the Nazis went berserk and attacked Poland, our old friend turned everything he and his first wife possessed into jewellery and just enough into money to buy passages to safety in South Africa.

Jewellery is portable and good for value in any city. The wife could cook. If she made chocolates, he could sell them. They needed money to get started. Borrow some? They were strangers, so without credit. They could sell the jewellery, true. With a war coming, though, it would gain value as time went by. Much better use it to get some credit—as security for a loan.

Good jewellery being about the best sort of security, they got the loan of money at a modest rate of interest, started up, worked like beavers and prospered. Before long, world war helped a lot by cutting down supplies of chocolates and other sweets from Britain and Europe where most of them had come from hitherto. In no time they had a flourishing little business, which gave them excellent credit for borrowing more money from the bank.

Thanks to the war, all sorts of goods which used to flow in from Britain and Europe became hard to get, and he made the most of it. Getting around the way he did and always had, with his eyes and ears wide open, he kept finding out who wanted what where, and where to get it—especially in the way of luxury goods like furs, cosmetics, clothes, expensive food and drink—the sort of things rich people need to show off with; the sort of things a wide boy could make 'a real killing' with; that's to say, a huge profit. And when it came to making 'killings' he had few equals; over the years he had become very artful at persuading people with things to sell that they weren't worth much, and getting others to think they were getting them cheap for three or four times as much and would be thought pretty poor and so be looked down on if they didn't have them.

At the same time, he 'invested' a lot of time and energy—especially his wife's—in getting his name and picture often in the newspapers helping to entertain soldiers on their way to the battlefields in Egypt and elsewhere. When the war ended, he was rich and given much credit for having done so much to win it.

So far, what he had done really was invest his own skill, time, energy and credit in hiring other people's credit and skills to fetch and carry goods, pay and collect his dues, keep tallies of his business deals, and publicize him one way and another, and he had got quite rich in the process. Quite rich. Not really rich. Nothing like as rich as some people. To be really rich, he knew, you didn't just *hire* other people's skills; you owned rights to use them. Instead of buying and selling *goods*, in other words, you bought and sold *companies*. What are companies, after all, but collections of 'plant' (buildings, machinery, etc.) and skills? What are skills, after all, but tools? What are employees but tools? What are companies, after all, but tools—tools for making or doing this or that, hence tools for drawing value from? Obviously, to be really rich, you must own companies, not just things. You must deal in companies, not just things.

So he took to investing all his time, energy and credit in 'securities'—that's to say 'rights' of one sort or another to draw value in 'dues' and 'dividends' from industrial and commercial concerns of various kinds. In other words, he took to buying and selling stocks and shares and bonds. Stocks are IOUs of a kind: whoever holds them is entitled to get interest every year from the people who issued them, and sooner or later the 'face-value' in cash. Bonds are much the same. Shares are different. They're not IOUs. A shareholder owns a bit of the right to control the management of a company and pocket a part of the profit it makes—among other things.

As a kind of property, this right to control a company is usually 'diced', so to speak, into lots of little standard-sized 'cubes', called 'shares', which are bought and sold in batches or quantities like, well, tablets—anything one buys in quantities—dozens, hundreds, or, for that matter, thousands. If you own all or most of the shares of (or in) a company, you can do pretty well what you like with it regardless . . . as long as it's 'alive'—'a going concern'.

Regardless? Within the Law, of course.

Anyway, what he could he did. What he did, on the whole, was much like what second-hand dealers in furniture do—buy up worn bits, get skilled people to do them up, then flog them. Mind you, companies are machines of a kind for producing profits, so, while he bought and sold 'control' of some, he kept it of others. . . . And as the years went by he put together a sizable collection or 'portfolio' of 'controlling rights' in well over a hundred concerns, and became *really* rich: and also became, thanks largely to the pilot, quite widely known as 'Old Blubberguts', which was near enough to his real name to catch people's fancy.

Incidentally, somewhere along his way to wealth and fame, that first wife of his died. They'd never had children; there wasn't time. So she'd devoted herself heart and soul to his career.

For years he'd seen little of her. He'd been so busy—all over the place—they'd become almost strangers. She'd failed to rise with him, remained more or less the kitchen-maid she'd been when he married her—*without* the face or figure.

Now, oddly enough, sitting under that aircraft wing, it was that girl he suddenly remembered, as he held the great diamond in his hands. Telling her long ago that she was worth far more to him than anything else could ever be. What was that saying about the price of a virtuous woman being above rubies? Above this or any diamond. Price? . . . Merit, more likely.

Getting—and staying—really rich had left him so little time for anything else. Fun, for instance, for *spending* the loot. Riches, after all, are for spending. On fun? What else? The pilot was a fool—or was he? He had fun—plenty of it by all accounts. On his mere pittance. What wouldn't *he* do with the diamond or rather what it would fetch—a tenth of what it would fetch—back in civilization?

4 Means. That's a useful word. Means. Yes. In the Forsyte Era 'well-to-do' people were people 'of ample means'. Others were 'of modest' or 'moderate means'. Then there were people 'without means'—*private* means, that's to say—people who were 'dependent on earnings' (rather contemptibly). Really rich people, by the way, didn't have means: they had 'great fortunes'—'possessions'—or 'estates'.

Means. Means equals tools equals properties of one kind or another. Means—to what end? Independence, of course. People were talked of as being 'of independent means'. 'So-and-so—a gentleman (or lady) of independent means.' Means to please yourself and to do what you liked, when you liked, where you liked and pretty well how you liked. Nobody gave *them* orders. Anyone who tried 'presumed'—an unforgivable offence. 'Do you presume, sir, to tell *me* what to do? You are a cad, sir'—a cad being the opposite of a gentleman—hence a man without means. Whatever else a gentleman might lack, he had to have 'means'. He couldn't afford to be caught earning a living.

Mind you, the Forsyte-type did tend to earn livings—the men—anyway—in or near that ancient, honourable and most comfortable of clubs, the City—as merchants of tea, wool, rubber, metals, textiles and similar commodities, or as brokers of stocks, shares, bills, freights, bullion, 'foreign exchange' and goodness knows what else, or as solicitors or bankers. In other words, they invested their credit in commodities with an eye to making profits, or in 'know-how' with an eye to pocketing fees or commissions—and (most important of all, perhaps) in 'know-who'. They belonged to the right clubs, lived in the right places and mixed with the right people—people, that's to say, who tended to be in the know and could push business their way. And the returns and revenues they got from these shrewd investments in credit and connections enabled them in their heyday to live very comfortably indeed. But being above all prudent, they didn't overdo the living. They salted a tidy proportion of their revenues away in other kinds of properties for the sake of their *future value* as much as for the revenues they would or should yield—in land and

OH I DO HAVE A FEW LITTLE POSSESSIONS -ESTATES- DON'T YOU KNOW - THAT SORT OF THING
I HAVE A FEW LITTLE ASSETS: SECURITIES, PROPERTY HOLDINGS, INVESTMENTS IN TRUST.
I JUST HAVE A JOB!
INDEPENDENT MEANS
MODERATE MEANS
MEAN

Means. . . .

buildings and promising shares, not to mention the best kinds of IOUs—Government loan stocks, debentures (loan stocks) of solid companies, and mortgage loans 'secured' on land and buildings likely to be in lasting demand. Everything they bought had to be good—solid—of the best materials—likely to keep and perpetually gain value. And they insured everything with great care. Whatever might happen to any one of their businesses or of their investments, they made as sure as possible by 'diversifying'—by balancing swings against roundabouts—that the family fortunes would still float and flourish.

After all, you could never make 100 per cent sure. The best families were apt to produce their fools—black sheep—even rogues. The daughters, of course, were the main headache: the females. All impulse, as often as not, and no sense—no business sense, anyway. Easy meat for 'adventurers'—men without means, expectations or prospects. You had to provide for them of course, but you couldn't possibly trust them with *Capital.* So what you did was to invest chunks of Capital for them in the safest kinds of IOUs—'gilt-edged' (Government) stocks, for preference—which could be relied on, you reckoned, to yield a steady cash income for ever. You put the securities—that's to say, the Capital—in the hands of family trustees with instructions to pay the income from them—the interest—to the 'beneficiaries', but keep that Capital well and truly in family hands at any cost.

In a nutshell, they invested for girls mainly in money, which, years later, cost many of their poor daughters very dear in value. In that heyday of the 'Forsytes' it was unthinkable that British money could ever lose value. Great Britain, after all, owned most of the world's gold, silver and copper—and most of the mines, not to mention the deposits, of those precious metals. Her credit was vast and, surely, inexhaustible? Britannia ruled the waves.

5 Most people don't have one-track minds so they don't want to be either rich misers or tycoons. Being a 'Forsyte' type was great fun for some of them, no doubt—the ones who *spent* the money on 'doing their own things', but not so much for the ones who spent their *lives* collecting the properties. They didn't own the stuff, you might say. It owned them. An old Hindu once said to me, 'You can't own property, you can only be owned *by* it'. There's a lot in that; and it's all right, I dare say,

if you can opt out and exist happily under a bo-tree, being One with Nature. Most of us can't though. We have to make out in the organized world: and making out in that without any property at all is as good as impossible. At any rate, it's not so funny. And I suppose it's fair to say that if one has to live in the organized world, one should get as much harmless fun and as little avoidable woe out of life as one can. Which calls for collecting a modest pile of value to meet the costs of getting the fun and avoiding the woe, without becoming a slave to the job of collecting—and keeping the pile. At least that's the way I see it.

Now, if you start from scratch, your only properties, as I've already said, are your wits and your muscles. These are your only 'assets' (which is yet another word for properties or tools). Your first task then is to create as high a 'market-price' for them as you can. This means acquiring skill or skills which are in demand *and then publicizing it or them.* Make no mistake about this.You may acquire more skill in some line than most or a particular kind of skill—as a performer of some kind—that nobody else has; but if hardly anybody knows about it, it can have little or no market-value however highly you may price it yourself. You may shrink from the idea of publicizing yourself; most people do because they're afraid of spiteful remarks from jealous acquaintances. Also, they've probably been taught that modesty is a virtue. So what? Virtues are assets which help to get you liked and trusted and can help to raise your market-value, but only if they are publicized. The more people get to hear well of your skills and virtues, the higher your market-value will rise. So your modesty is a handicap to you, though it's a great help, of course, to others who want to hire your skill, i.e. to employers. Employers, remember, are 'users': that's what the word means.

Naturally they want to pay as little as they can for the skills they hire—as little as hirelings will accept. Demand is what creates market-value, but there can be no demand without fame and no fame without publicity. Which is why Oscar Wilde wrote, 'If there's one thing in the world worse than being talked about, it's not being talked about.' Fame *means* being talked about.

Skill and fame are properties—the first properties a poor man should invest in. By 'fame' I mean reputation, being known—well known—for skilfulness in your line to the people who need your kind of skill.

How do you make a reputation? Seldom, oddly enough, by simply being very skilful. Being very skilful certainly helps, and you may be 'discovered' by chance, though it's unlikely. What you have to do is make—and keep—yourself and your skills conspicuous among the *right* people—the people who could use your skills—*in such a way that they will want to hire you.* Obviously what you want is a good reputation, not a bad one!

A good reputation is the one property you can't buy simply with money. To get it, you'll certainly have to spend—that's to say invest—some cash, but mainly what you'll have to invest is some of your time and energy in publicity.

Reputation is a kind of property which can contain great value. Publicity is the tool for getting it. Showmanship is the tool for getting publicity. You can be an effective showman without money: in fact, if you have little or no money, skill in showmanship is one of the most important skills you can acquire.

Showmanship is an art like music, medicine, teaching, farming, mining and so on: like investing for that matter. Within every art there are scores of particular techniques with particular tools for doing particular jobs.

Showmanship is a complicated art. You don't have to be an *expert* showman yourself, though, to make good use of it, any more than you have to be an expert doctor to make good use of medicine. If necessary, you can hire the skills of an expert showman—if you can afford it. Most celebrities do, or people half way to celebrity. For beginners, though, it is a matter of do-it-yourself.

Here are a few hints. Think out carefully answers to these questions (your aim, remember, is to increase the market-value of your skills).

1 Who are the people who could hire my skills?
2 Where are they?
3 How could I draw their attention to my skills and get them to want them?

The first two questions usually call simply for some home-work. The third is much the trickiest.

You can advertise. This is the worst way: people rather disbelieve boasts. You can get others to advertise you. This is a bit better, but not much. And both ways cost money. Much the best way is to get into the news—in the right way—

You can advertise

at the right time—in the right columns; that's to say the ones read by the right people. Or get talked about in the right way among the right people.

In either case, you must 'make news'. To 'make news' you must either do something new or novel and get it reported, or do something ordinary in a novel way and get it reported.

Doing can be saying—saying something novel or saying something ordinary in a novel way—and getting either reported.

This little book is about investing with money rather than with time and energy, though you'll have to use all three. (Remember the old saying 'Time *is* money'.) To invest well you have to spend time and energy and money. To start with you'll have to spend time and energy to get as much money as you can to invest with. This means getting as much money for your skills as you can: that's to say, selling your skills. The art of selling is nine-tenths the art of showmanship. In a nutshell:

1 Buy or borrow from your local library a book or two on salesmanship, marketing and public relations. Study them carefully and plan how to 'market' your skills.
2 Don't be shy. Don't be modest about your skills—your abilities. About your virtues, yes—but not about your skills. This is *false* modesty. People take each other very largely as they take *money*, at face-value. If you *say* or imply that your skills aren't up to much, people won't attach much value to them. You must show them off. To the right people, in the right places, in the right ways, at the right times.

Only when you've *got* reputation can you afford to be modest. It's the same with wealth. Once you're rich, you can afford to look poor, but not before. As Oliver Goldsmith said, 'The best way to stay poor is to look poor.' You need all the face-value you can get.

Plenty of poor skills fetch high prices thanks to good showmanship. That goes for all goods—including of course securities. Especially securities. You can partly gauge the usefulness of most goods you can see, hear, feel, smell or taste—with those senses. To gauge the usefulness of skills and securities, you have to use your wits. Gumption, mainly. Above all, gumption. Common sense.

6 So you're getting as much money as you can for your skills.

Much of it is bound to get spent on the business of living—on necessities, amenities, comforts, on fun. Amenities, comfort and fun are near-necessities: what kind and how much of each is up to you. You need some cash in hand or handy, for emergencies. What's left you should spend on investments to get your *future* amenities, comfort and fun. How much depends on how much you're prepared to forgo *now* in the way of amenities, comfort and fun.

Future value to be got from an investment is called 'return'.

Some investments can give 'return' in two ways—in 'yield' *and* 'profit'. Others can only give a 'return' in *either* yield *or* profit.

Yield is like a crop. If you buy an acre of meadow, it will yield you long grass every summer, which can be fed to cattle to produce saleable milk and beef. If you sell the land after a few years, it may fetch more money than you gave for it—a profit in money though not necessarily in value. The 'return' from the investment is the added-up yields of each year plus the profit or minus the loss—whether in money or value—though it's only the value, or course, that matters.

Our tycoon's diamond is an example of the kind which usually produces no yield but is as good as certain to gain value when money is fast losing it and seems certain to go on losing it. Why? Because the demand for such 'valuables' grows simply because so many other types of investment are likely to lose value. This kind of investment is often called a 'lock-up' because it tends to hold fast the value it has and gains. Many works of art and antiques come into the same class, their main snags being that they can be faked or damaged and are apt to go in and out of fashion. Gems are almost damage-proof, can be tested and stay in fashion. Most 'valuables' are liable to get stolen.

Mind you, yield—i.e. income—*can* be got from such properties by hiring them out, but it's obviously a difficult and risky business. The best examples of pure lock-ups are, say, bars or ingots of precious metals which are useless in that form and can't be hired out. The snag about them is that they have to be kept safe somewhere (which may cost money) and they do lose as well as gain value from time to time.

Most people want income-producing investments rather than 'lock-ups', if only because they want a regular 'yield' to spend on necessities, plus amenities, comforts and fun while the going's good, so to speak. Shrewd investors go in for so much of 'income-producers' and so much of 'lock-ups'. The ideal investment, of course, is one that bids fair to produce *increasing* yield and fat profit—the fatter the merrier. There's no investment that *will*. There can be no 'dead cert'.

Since this is the ideal investment, though, it's the sort everybody's after. And since it's the likely yield (income) in *future* that people are primarily after, it's this mainly that makes its market-price what it is *now*—high because everyone's after it. And that means there's not likely to be much profit to be got from selling it later on. The price now tends, as the pros put it, to 'discount future growth'.

What's more—*and this is where you have to be specially careful*—gains in *money*-yields and *money*-prices may well mask losses of value, simply because money may have lost value faster than the yield and price have gained it so far.

If this proves to be the case, you may well pocket a lot more pounds, dollars, marks or what-have-you than you invested, but a lot fewer of the 'Vals' which count. You'll have lost, in fact.

And what this means is that where you 'put money into' any income-producing investment, you must try to gauge not just the return in money but the return in value.

And this means you'll have to guess (or 'guesstimate') in advance how fast money will lose value while you hold the property in question.

We'll come to this again, often, when talking about different kinds of income-producing investments and securities. First of all, let's try to classify them as simply as possible.

7 Yield comes from different kinds of property under various names: from land and buildings as 'rent': from deposits, loans and loan stocks as 'interest': from ordinary shares as 'dividends': from patents and copyrights and other rights as 'royalties'. Fares, fees, tolls and dues are paid for the use of such properties as skills and facilities of one kind or another.

It all sounds horribly confusing and *is*. However, it's not so bad for a start once you realize that investing is merely buying some kind of property and that there are basically only two kinds: 'tangible' and 'intangible'.

Tangible properties are 'concrete' things like land, buildings, machines, vehicles, commodities, 'valuables'. Some of them you can hire out for income easily, some with difficulty, some not at all.

Intangibles are rights, 'abstract' things which give their holders a claim of some sort on other people's property. Rights have to be set out on bits of paper (documents) known as 'securities'.

The holder of a security has the right to claim payment of dues from somebody or some body under conditions set out in the document.

Most rights are 'transferable'—can be passed, that's to say, from one owner to another, sold, bequeathed or given away. Some aren't. Some securities are registered. Some are 'bearer': whoever holds these, registered or not, can claim the dues 'on presentation'.

To get this clear let's look at things from the other end for the moment.

You can't set up or run any kind of business whether it's a shop, factory, school, hospital or even government without money in some form: what's called 'capital'—capital or 'common' stock—a *stock* that's to say of credit: a stock of the stuff to draw upon to buy materials and equipment, to pay wages, salaries, rent, rates, light, heat, taxes and so on.

If you haven't got enough yourself already, you must get a supply of it from other people, just as you have to get a supply of electricity, fuel, raw materials, etc., from other people. Credit, in short, is *the* key—'raw material' for *all* kinds of organized business.

Credit, as a raw material, 'occurs', so to speak, only in the pockets or bank balances of people—of Tom, Dick and Harry. You can only get it out of them by begging it (as charities do) by borrowing it (hiring), by swapping something for it (selling), by winning it (betting)—or, of course, by stealing it.

Private and public enterprises don't, as a rule, go in (openly at any rate) for begging, betting or stealing. They either hire credit or sell 'rights': governments, of course, levy it by taxation, but they also 'borrow'.

To get a supply of 'credit', businesses must offer something in return either direct to the public or to the 'institutions'—banks or insurance and pension funds—which collect it in dribs and drabs from the public and 'stock' it in large quantities. These institutions are in fact 'stockists of credit'. Businesses which want to borrow (hire) credit, offer a rate of interest for so many years or indefinitely. They give those who lend to them some kind of certificate, bond or receipt which entitles the holder to claim the interest at intervals and have the face-value back some time in the future. If they don't want to borrow, they offer shares and issue certificates to buyers.

So there are really only two kinds of financial investment—and both are 'claims on stock'.

Simple enough—in principle. Quite. What makes it so complicated *in practice* is all the permutations and combinations—that's to say possible 'assortments'—of different rights. People who buy 'stock' in a business—loan or share stock—stake claims either on its earnings or its assets (plant, machinery, equipment, and so on) or on both. But they queue up for payment according to the kind of rights they own. Loan stockholders come before shareholders, for instance, and 'preference' shareholders before 'ordinary' shareholders. If the earnings of the business are only just enough to pay the loan stock interest, there's nothing left for the shareholders, pref. or ordinary, and the ordinary shareholders come last of all in any queue. In any one business, there may be several grades of loan stock. But while the people in front of the ordinary shareholders get a *fixed* rate of interest, the ordinary shareholders at the back may get a dividend or share-out of much of what's left, and this can be a very fat rake-off if earnings are very large. What's more, if the earnings look like getting bigger and bigger, the market-price of a company's shares tends to go up and up, while that of its loan stocks stays very much the same or even goes down. So the return (yield plus profit) from an ordinary share can be far, far higher than from any grade of fixed-interest loan stock. *Can* be. . . . But since you've no claim on the 'par', i.e. face-value, of ordinary shares, you *can* lose your shirt owning those of a company which goes bankrupt, i. e. dies. If you have some of its loan stock, you may get something from the sale of its assets.

So on the face of it, the *safest* investment is in top grade loan stock of a concern which can get credit when it wants it. Governments can get it from taxes, and huge corporations can usually 'raise' it easily (at a price) from institutions, the public, or even from the Government. *On the face of it, though*. . . . Investments in loan stocks are investments in *money*.

So, to be worth buying, any kind of loan stock must offer you a future return, yield plus profit, when you sell it or collect its face-value, which will leave you then with more *value* (after you've paid taxes) than you'll have spent on buying it in the first place. And any share must obviously, in the same way, offer you a likely chance of a bigger return still—quite a lot bigger—enough to offset the bigger risks of loss which come from being last in the queue.

8 Keep asking yourself (I'm sorry to keep harping on this, but I must) what you're investing for. You see, 'investment opportunities' are much like goods in a shop. Different 'shapes', 'sizes' and 'styles' are designed to suit different kinds of people with different needs. Some will suit pretty well anyone up to a point, some only special kinds of people in special circumstances. The snag is there's no such thing as an investments shop. There's not even a single market with various 'stalls' in it. You simply have to decide what you want, keep your eyes skinned, and get advice; though you need to be wary about advice because the number of real experts is very small indeed. There are plenty of people about who know quite a bit about this *kind* or that but *only* this or that; and with the best will in the world, any of them may mislead you thanks to his limitations.

Ask yourself, then—do I just want to put my spare cash to work when I have some? Would I want it back at short notice? Am I out to collect enough value in so many weeks, months or years to buy something—a car, a caravan, a cabin-cruiser, a house, a business or part of one? Do I want to build up enough 'private means' to yield me so much a year of my own—someday? If so, when?

Remember, the bigger the target and the shorter the time you give yourself to reach it, the bigger the risks you'll have to take and the more time, effort and skill you'll have to put into the job.

Most people go in for a bit of 'casual' investing—they keep the odd spot of cash in a 'savings account' which earns some interest and can be drawn out more of less at the drop of a hat. Many use 'savings' or 'deposit accounts' also to build up some short-term target sum—to pay for next summer's holidays or Christmas festivities. All too many, I may say, prefer to get these things on tick—'credit terms'—h. p.—and pay, if they only knew it, through the nose for the loan. 'Credit' of this kind is generally a plain extravagance. Shrewd people only borrow to get hold, sooner or later, of more value. Suppose you're going to need £100 for next year's holiday. You borrow the money at 20 per cent per annum or more. If you take a year to pay off the loan, your holiday will have cost you far more than £100. If, instead, you save and invest £10 per month for ten months the holiday will cost you less than £100: the interest will pay for part of it. Obviously? Yes, but how many people forget or don't realize it?

For these 'short-term targets', or when you want to keep spare cash busy, the right investment 'media', as they call them, are these 'savings' and 'deposit accounts', with the National Savings Bank or any of the 'clearing' or Trustee Savings Banks or Building Societies: or, if you've got £100 or more to spare, you can sometimes lend it to a local authority and get it back at short notice.

There are, then, four main questions to ask when 'shopping' —considering this or that.

1 What's the rate of interest I can get?
2 How much notice do I have to give to get the cash back again?
3 What's the smallest sum I can deposit? Must it be a sizable lump sum? Or can I put in a small regular sum? Or just odd spots of cash when I can or feel like it?
4 What are the risks?

The National Savings Bank, the clearing banks, the Trustee Savings Banks and the good building societies all take small, regular or 'casual' deposits and pay out cash 'on demand' or at a week or two's notice. And with most of them your money's as safe as it can be.

Broadly speaking, the shorter the term you're willing to leave your money 'on deposit' with any of these, the lower the rate of interest it'll pay you. The reason is simple: 'institutions' are run by shrewd people, so they're mostly going to hire your money at a rate (price) which will leave them room to use it to their own advantage—that's to say get more *value* with it than they pay you—with as little risk as possible. What's more, it's costly for them to deal in dribs and drabs. The bigger the sum and the longer they can keep it, the more room they have for investing it safely and profitably themselves.

Nobody, or hardly anybody, ever offers to hire your credit (money) to do you *personally* a bit of good—to pay you more, anyway, than he, she or it must to tempt you to stump up. No, not even Authority. What they're nearly all out for is the better of the bargain with you—in *value*—whether for their own good or, as they see it, for some community's. So it's up to you to look after yourself.

Because of inflation (depreciation of money) few, if any, 'deposit' investments are likely to return you more *value* than you spend on them; in most cases, definitely *less*. They're merely likely to do better for you than no investment at all. Unless, that is, you're liable for a lot of surtax, in which case this little book's unlikely to be of much interest to you anyway.

9 Another thing I can tell you about 'Old Blubberguts', he never let a penny lie idle for a day if he could help it. What's more, when he needed money in any form, he 'hired' it for as little as possible or borrowed it for nothing and kept it as long as he could. (He never paid a bill until he had to.) 'Where there's a deal', he was fond of saying, 'there's a profit'—'for the smart boy,' he meant—which means, of course, there's a loss for some mug or victim.

Mind you, unless you feel you must, I wouldn't urge you to be 'on the make' to that extent: it's apt to get you widely underloved. However, there's no point in going to the other extreme and being the mug all, most or even much of the time. It's foolish to keep money lying idle, as I've said, in any form. Everybody, though, has to have some cash handy for casual expenses, paying bills and coping with emergencies. How much? Well that's up to you, of course, but as a coarse measure, what adds up to, say, a sixth of your annual income.

'Keep a sixth liquid', Forsyte-types used to say; 'liquid' meaning either as cash or in a form of investment easily turned into cash at a moment's or very short notice. Easily 'realizable', as they say.

Suppose your income were £2,100 a year. A sixth of that would be £350 (I'm ignoring 'deductions' by the way). You'd be unlikely to want all or even most of that suddenly. Probably, you'd agree, a tenner's usually enough to have on you in 'tokens', but you'd want to be able to lay your hands at the drop of a hat on, say, £40 without keeping it 'idle'. The remaining £300 you'd be unlikely to need at less than a fortnight's or even a month's notice.

Right. There are several ways of keeping cash busy, handy and safe. The National Savings Bank offers you various facilities. So do the Trustee Savings Banks and the Building Societies. And, of course, there are the big clearing banks.

What you do is either 'deposit' money with (i. e. hire it out to) one of these institutions or buy from it shares or units of 'stock' of some kind. These 'institutions' guarantee i.e. undertake to pay you so much in 'interest'—'dividends'—'return'—'bonus', and repay your deposit or 'redeem' (buy back) the shares or stock units 'on demand' or at so much notice—at face-value. Make a note of that 'face-value'. They're apt—the National Savings people especially—to talk of or imply *value* when they mean face-value which, as you well know now, is a very different thing. (Oddly enough, there's a law against this kind of artfulness.) However, unless you leave money a long time, many months at least, invested in this way, the loss of value's unlikely to be very much: and if value did look like gushing out in 'runaway inflation', you could, if you were brisk enough, get your money out and quickly swap it for something else—but that's really another story.

Let's take the NSB first. It's run by the Government and works through 20,000 and more branch SBPO's, which makes it easily the most convenient. You can 'deposit' by 'opening' an 'ordinary account' at any branch with as little as 25 p. At present* you'll get interest at the rate of 3½ per cent a year on each complete pound you have in the account for a full calendar month. You won't have to pay income tax on interest up to £21 (which will accrue to a balance of £600 *kept in for a year*). As long as your balance is big enough, you can draw up to £20 in cash from it by simply handing your bank-book into any SBPO. If you need more, you can usually get it fairly quickly—in a day or two. This Bank charges you nothing for keeping your account. And your money (face-value) is safe because, after all, the Government prints the stuff. Once and as long as you have £50 in an ordinary account, you can open an 'investment' account, that's to say 'deposit', but be unable to get *any* of your money out without a month's notice. You have to put in at least £1, and, at present, this Bank'll pay you interest at the rate of 7½ per cent a year, but none of this interest is free of income-tax.

This point about income-tax is very important, of course. If you have to pay anything between a third and a half of the interest back to the Government in income-tax, you won't

* January 1972.

get 7½ per cent—you'll get something between 5 per cent and 3¾ per cent, which is better, to be sure, than 3½ per cent—but then you've got that month's notice to give before you can draw anything out. There's no simple rule-of-thumb calculation, unfortunately, as rates of income-tax vary from person to person. A word of warning, however. The NSB and Building Societies, who are after your money, love putting up posters announcing some lofty interest rate or other with a small-print note under or alongside saying that this is what their *real* rate of interest is 'equal to' or 'the equivalent of'. So it is—in a sense. 'If you're liable for income tax at the *full* standard rate, then you'd have to get *this* high rate of interest from others which is *not* income-tax free to keep what you do keep if you accept *our* (lower) rate which *is* income-tax free.' That's what they're saying! This is much the same as a four-foot man shouting 'I'm as tall as any six-footer', then mumbling 'when any six-footer's sitting down'. All that matters to you, needless to say, is how much interest *you*—not others—are going to be allowed to *keep* by the Government.

You can get exactly the same deposit facilities from any of the eighty or so Trustee Savings Banks as from the NSB but they only have some 1,500 branch offices between them (in the bigger towns) so they're nowhere near so convenient as the NSB with its 20,000-plus SB post offices.

Unlike the NSB, building societies and clearing banks, TSBs are run solely in the interest of their depositors, and your money's as safe with them as with the N S B, since they can only invest depositors' money in government securities. For practical purposes, they are a part of the Government's National Savings set-up.

Building societies, however, exist to lend money to would-be house-owners, which they can only do by borrowing it from others. They're not profit-seeking set-ups but they do cost money to run, so the rate of interest they can pay to depositors has to be quite a bit less than they can expect to get from borrowers—the people they make mortgage loans to. They do have competitors—insurance companies, for instance—so their rates to borrowers vary as 'money-market' rates vary. As a result, anyway, the deposit rates they offer you (which vary from society to society) are apt to go up and down—quite suddenly, at times.

You can open either a 'share account' or a 'deposit account' with any of close on 500 different building societies

—with as little as £1. With a 'share' account you become a member of the society and get a slightly higher rate of interest than from a 'deposit' account, because you're taking slightly more risk. If the society 'died', depositors' claims on its assets would rank before those of its shareholders. At the present time* you can get interest at 4¾ per cent a year on share accounts and 4½ per cent on deposit accounts from the best Building Societies with numerous branches, and a shade more from others which offer less convenience. Since income-tax has already been paid by the society (by special arrangement), you keep the lot unless you're liable for surtax. Anything you put in earns interest from the day you put it in to the day you draw it out, and you can put some in or take some out pretty well when you like.

So a share account with a good building society certainly does you prouder than an NSB ordinary account as far as interest goes, and as proud as the NSB investment account *if you're liable for much income-tax*. But it's less convenient (there are far more Savings Bank post offices open six days a week till teatime or so than any building society has branches) —and there's rather more possibility of a drop in any building society's interest rates. Then there's the hint of risk; though that you can disregard as far as 'handy cash' deposits are concerned with any good building society—one that belongs to the Building Societies Association or has 'trustee status'.

Lastly, or almost lastly—there are the clearing banks. The point to bear in mind about these is this. Unlike the NSB, TSBs or BSs, their job is to make profits for ordinary shareholders, and they do this mostly by lending money. They'll 'look after' your money for you and pay sums for you to others when you 'issue' written 'orders'—e.g. cheques. This they'll do if you open a 'current' account—at a price: that's to say, they'll usually charge you for it. They'll also take your money 'on deposit' paying you interest at the rate of 2 per cent a year less than Bank Rate set by Government, which varies from time to time. None of this interest, though, is free of income-tax (or surtax) and you have to give, as a rule, two weeks' notice before you can withdraw any money from a clearing bank 'deposit' account.

No single clearing bank has anything like as many branches as the NSB; they all shut anyway from 3 p.m. and don't open on Saturday at all, so they're a lot less convenient.

* January 1972.

Another thing; you can't just walk into any branch (unless you have a credit card—which is apt to be costly) and draw cash out of it. You have to have a 'cashing arrangement', The truth is that while these banks offer many useful services, there's not much point in your having a clearing bank account, current or deposit, unless you're likely to want to be able to borrow from the bank from time to time. It can be distinctly expensive and the cost needs watching.

What this all adds up to is that the NSB offers in its ordinary account much the best terms and service for keeping cash busy but easily got at. Its investment account also wins hands down on convenience, but you can get a better 'net' (after tax) yield from a share account with any worthwhile building society if you're liable for income-tax at the full standard rate. All but the biggest building societies are comparatively inconvenient unless you live close to a branch. The TSBs offer you the same terms as the NSB but even the best of them aren't in the same street for convenience as the NSB.

So here's the best way to start investing:

1 Go to the nearest Savings Bank Post Office and get the latest leaflets about National Giro and the National Savings Bank. Study them carefully.
2 Open a National Giro account at this Post Office. £1 will do.
3 Arrange for your pay to be put direct into this National Giro account, or put it there yourself.
4 Open an ordinary account with the NSB (25p will do), and give the National Giro a standing order to pay so much a week or month into this NSB 'ordinary' account—and go on doing so until there's £50 in it. . . . This will qualify you to open an NSB 'investment' account—if it suits you, which may or may not be the case.

NB By the way. . . . Be wary—very wary—of advertisements offering *higher* interest rates to depositors. By 'higher' I mean noticeably higher than any well-known building society's. No 'finance house' or other organization can pay you and others fancy interest rates without taking biggish risks with the money it attracts: which means a bigger risk for depositors, as a rule, than the extra interest is worth—much bigger.

Offers of higher-than-usual interest rates have tempted from time to time millions of gullible or hard-pressed depositors into grief and sorrow.

10 And your next step? Well, this depends on interest rates (which vary from time to time) and how much income-tax you're liable for as time goes on. You remember my saying there's no harm in keeping a 'reserve' of cash or near-cash equal roughly to a sixth of your annual income? Two months' pay—after deductions. Well, with £50 in Giro and £50 in an NSB ordinary account, that's £100 of it. The rest of your sixth you should put, if you pay only low-rate income-tax—or none—into an NSB investment account (or TSB 'special investment' account): but if you pay some income-tax at the full standard rate, it'll pretty certainly pay you to put it into a good building society share account. Quite apart from convenience, you have to give that month's notice to draw cash from an NSB investment account whereas you can get cash pronto from your building society—provided, admittedly, there's a branch handy.

A very important thing about either is that any money you pay into it earns interest from the day you put it in to the day you draw it out. It's never idle. With plenty of 'fixed interest' investments, though, this isn't so. Savings Certificates, for instance. If you buy these, you have to hold them for so many months before they qualify for interest. What you want from your 'liquid reserve' is cash at short—at worst a month's—notice—with interest regardless.

If you're aiming to buy a house one of these days, you should definitely plump for the building society, because a decent share balance there will get you a good place in its queue for mortgage loans when you come to want one. As far as that goes, if and when you see the time coming when you may want to borrow money from a clearing bank, it'll pay you to start keeping some cash on deposit with one of these. There's a great deal a clearing bank can do for you when you're up and coming; its goodwill is worth buying, but it's apt to be wasteful to use one when you're a beginner.

O K for keeping cash handy but busy? Right. Now let's look at 'investment targets'.

2 Test Yourself Questions

1 What 'assets' are you born with? What are assets? How can you go about getting as much value as possible from them? [Section 5]

2 What is 'return'? What use are 'lock-up' investments? What are their chief advantages and drawbacks? What is meant by 'discounting future growth'? [Section 6]

3 How many different kinds of 'yield' can you think of? What are 'tangible' and 'intangible' properties? What is capital? What are the two basic kinds of financial investment? What is a security? [Section 7]

4 What are the main differences between loan stocks and ordinary shares? What are the advantages of holding (*a*) loan stocks (*b*) ordinary shares, and what are the main disadvantages? [Section 7]

5 What are the right investment media for keeping money handy but busy? What four questions should you ask before choosing? [Section 8]

6 Which is the most convenient 'deposit' medium? Why? What is the best way to start investing? Why should you beware of offers of high interest rates? What is 'high'? [Section 9]

7 What *special* reasons are there for considering depositing with a building society or clearing bank? [Section 10]

3 Gaining—and Losing

1 Investing, you know, is really a kind of adventuring. When you make an investment of any kind, you go on a venture. There's no such thing as a 'permanent' or 'perfectly safe' investment. There can't be. Why? Because value can't be caged.

This is no bad way of seeing it. For one thing, it makes it more interesting. Being a serious—a regular—investor is not unlike being an old-time knight errant. In quest of this elusive 'guerdon' of Value, you ride off, so to speak, into mysterious Investmentland—a land full of illusions, mirages, lurking perils, barons in castles, ogres even, hidden hoards of Value beset with traps cunningly baited for trespassers and mugs. It's by no means uncharted, this country, and there are plenty of signposts, not to mention guides. The signposts, though, are more often designed to tempt than tell, the charts are little better than sketch-maps, largely in code and cipher, and good guides with a real knowledge of the country beyond their own neighbourhoods are pretty rare—and coy. In short, to venture in there on your own, you need strength, skill, nerve and your wits about you always.

For the nervous and the diffident, there are, as it were, escorted coach-expeditions: trusts and funds of one kind or another. These take parties on sensible safaris. You'll never make a 'killing' in any of these 'coaches'. Many of them, however, do offer you a comfortable ride to predictable, if modest, bags.

Predictable is a key word, where you have targets in mind. Targets act as landmarks to steer for, to save you wandering about aimlessly, going round in circles, blundering off after jack-o'-lanterns or siren songs into quagmires. Mind you, even coaches *can* break down, get driven off the road, or, for that matter, take you for a ride in more senses than one. There are coaches and coaches, not to mention drivers and drivers.

Anyway, targets. Most people's lives fall into certain phases: childhood; adolescence; bachelorhood; home-making; family-rearing; middle-age; retirement. Each adult phase demands means, predictable means. To get and equip the home: to educate and launch children: to buy or set up a

Investing is a kind of adventuring

business perhaps, or buy a partnership: to secure at least a decent livelihood in retirement. These are the big expenses one can make rough targets of, setting staging-posts, as it were, along the road. And one can make lesser targets of the costlier possessions one would like on the way—things one's unlikely to be able to write cheques for on the spur of the moment, short of landing a fairish pools win: those cars, caravans, cruisers, mink coats, dishwashers, luxury holidays, etc. As I said before, you can always get these things on 'credit terms' and get well and truly milked for the privilege. Where you must borrow—to buy a house, for instance—it'll still pay you to make a target of repaying the loan—to 'fund the debt' as they say, i.e. save and invest to build the sum up by the (future) 'redemption' date. It stands to reason. If you borrow £100 now and undertake to repay it in ten years' time, you'll be paying back the sum in face-value but probably far less in *value*: and if you invest the borrowed £100 now, you should, with luck, collect *more* value during the ten years. In the case of a house mortgage loan, you should get income-tax relief on loan interest, but we'll come to that later.

Meanwhile, for convenience sake, let's sort targets into short-term (up to two years away)—medium-short-term (two to five years away)—medium-long-term (five to twelve years off) and long-term (anything more than twelve years away). Naturally, you can make your own classes.

For short-term purposes, those NSB or TSB investment accounts and B S share accounts are as helpful as anything—if you *must* make the target or else. If you don't *have* to make the target, obviously you can take some risks. But then, if you didn't have to make a target, you wouldn't have one, come to think of it, would you? All I'm saying once more is that in practice it pays you hands down to set targets and to invest to pay for major things: you get so much more for your money. It goes so much further.

2 If you buy a £1 unit of the latest (Decimal) Issue of Government Savings Certificates, you can have £1.03 back after one year. That's 3 per cent interest—tax free; less though, than you'd get on £1 left for a year in an NSB ordinary or investment account. After two years you can get back £1.07½. That's an average of 3¾ per cent a year. After three years £1.15 (average 5 per cent a year). After four years £1.25 (average 6¼ per cent). All *simple* interest, incidentally. All tax-free.

It's typical of Government cunning these days in working out schemes to tempt you to leave your money in its hands for years at a time. It even claims that 'each unit grows in value'. What it should say is 'face-value'. If money leaks value at the rate of 5 per cent (simple) per year during the four years, the growth of value will average only 1¼ per cent and you certainly won't grow rich on that. Yes, the growth of 6¼ per cent a year in face-value is guaranteed, but there's no saying what the average rate of value-leakage may be over four years. It could well be more—a lot more—than 5 per cent.

Nor will you grow exactly rich (whatever they may say) by going in for SAYE, which is much the same sort of thing under a fancy new label. In this case, though, you undertake to pay at least £1 every month to the Government Department of National Savings for five years. At the end of the five years you get the face-value back plus a bonus of one year's savings (equivalent to an interest rate of just under 7 per cent a year compound), free of all tax. If, instead of claiming it, you leave this money with the Department for two more years, you get a bonus of two years' savings. That's quite a bit better as a rate than you can get with the Government Savings Certificate—*at the price of waiting*. If you want to withdraw your money from SAYE short of five years (and it's all or nothing), you'll get no interest at all if you do so during the first year, and only 2½ per cent a year compound (tax-free) up to the end of the fifth. If you stop contributing moreover but leave your savings in for the full five years, you'll only get interest on them at 4½ per cent a year compound (tax-free).

Those far-off 'carrots' of bonus look quite alluring till you remember they're face-value. Heaven only knows how much value will have leaked out of sterling money in five—not to mention seven—years' time. Moreover the 'stick' you get for dropping out of SAYE is fairly tough—when you see what you get elsewhere—by subscribing *regularly*, for instance, for shares of any good building society. At present you can get as much as 6 per cent a year (tax-free) from scratch on anything from 50p to £20 a month: and you can withdraw what you've saved plus accrued interest at any time 'on prior notice—without deduction or expense'. Mind you, the SAYE bonus is fixed and guaranteed once you've taken the plunge, whereas building society rates, as I've said before, are apt to vary as time goes by. Even so—what you've got with a BS subscription share deal is freedom of movement:

you're not 'locked in' by any penalty: you can switch to another investment at really short notice, while getting a good tax-free rate of interest from start to finish.

Freedom of movement in investment can be an important property in itself—terribly important.

I'd sooner go for subscription shares in a good building society, that is—a member of the BSA or, at any rate, one with trustee status; and I'd keep my eyes skinned for better interest rates and my hands as free as possible to switch *without* penalty. For one thing, if inflation speeds up, interest rates are bound to go up, because people who know their onions aren't going to lend their money and get less value back than they've lent if they can help it. It can be fatal to be 'locked in'. If you are, the only way out is by 'cutting your losses'; and that can be a very difficult thing to bring yourself to do.

One thing I'd *consider* doing is this. Building societies run SAYE accounts as well as share, subscription share and deposit accounts. If you pay lump sums of, say, £60 at intervals into a building society's share account, you can often arrange for it to transfer up to £10 a month into an SAYE account for you. This way you'll qualify for the SAYE tax-free bonus after five (or seven) years *and* get the tax-free interest as well on the balance while it's waiting in your share account for transfer to your SAYE account. This is a tidy, trouble-free way of getting nearly the best of both worlds.

Obviously you'll have to keep enough money in your BS share account for transfer. If £10 a month is to be transferred, each £60 will last for 6 months; if £5, for a year. If you're already having National Giro transfer part of your earnings regularly into an NSB ordinary account, you can simply arrange for the lump sum required to be transferred, when necessary, from your NSB ordinary account to your building society share account. By National Giro, by standing order. Only don't forget you've done it, if you do.

And don't forget that—even so—you won't get the best out of this arrangement unless you do stick with it for the full five or seven years.

3 So much for short-term and medium-short 'targets'. (Not that I'd make too much of short-term targets, myself: I'd simply aim to have a nice sum cooking away for me to be

You can open a share account with as little as £1

ready as soon as maybe.) Much more important are medium-long to long-term targets. Before I get on to 'coach-load' ways and means of hitting those, though, let's have another glance at the different *kinds* of investment securities. This'll help you to decide what 'coach-trips' can and can't do for you, not to mention a few other things.

Investment securities, like clothes, are offered in many styles. The ones we've just been talking about, for instance, promise you your money (face-value) back either 'on demand' or at 'some future date'. One or two of them promise to pay a certain rate or rates of interest, others don't. Some promise interest by the day, others only so much every four, six, or even twelve months. Out of these simple ingredients, you can make an almost endless range of 'recipes'. And then, of course, nobody has to promise face-value back—or interest—or 'yield' in any form. Government itself is really the only organization which *can* guarantee it because it makes the 'tokens' itself and stamps or prints the face-value on them. Government securities are 'tokens'—value-containers but *not* swapping-tools—as a rule. They leak value just as fast as money itself, but they also gain some for their holders in interest, growth, bonus, premium, or any other fancy name on the label.

What we talked about mainly was 'depositing'—letting money, you might call it, whether on 'overnight' terms or on short, medium or long lease. I mentioned one exception: the Decimal Savings Certificates.

A £1 Savings Certificate is really a miniature unit of Government loan stock of a special kind. Its face-value is repayable on demand and ownership of it can't be transferred to anyone else.

From time to time, for well over 200 years, Governments have been borrowing credit by 'issuing'—i.e. selling—stocks or bonds on various terms, in jumbo-size units of, usually, £100. Some issues are 'redeemable'—that's to say Government guarantees to repay the face-value at some future date: some are not. All bonds are redeemable. The total of Government debt is prodigious: it runs into tens of thousands of millions of pounds. And when some issue or other becomes due for 'redemption', the Government usually pays up not in cash but with another issue of stock or bonds. Unlike Saving Certificates, such stocks and bonds are 'transferable'—and quantities of them are freely bought and sold through the authorized Stock Exchanges. At prices which vary from time to time. Why?

It's a matter basically of how much yield people expect or hope to get and keep from this or that (kind of) investment. A huge industrial concern is offering to borrow at, say, 10 per cent a year, repaying 'principal' (face-value) in fifteen years' time. To attract lenders, Government would have to offer, say, 8 per cent (it can *guarantee* repayment and interest, whereas even the best industrial concern can fail—like Rolls-Royce). Then nobody will want an old—say 4 per cent—Government redeemable stock unless it will yield the same. So the market price of the £100 (face-value) units falls to £50, to offer buyers 8 per cent on their money.

Got it?

Mind you, that's over-simplified. Some day, Government will redeem that 4 per cent stock 'at par'—that's to say buy back all the units for the face-value of £100 each: so if you buy units for less than £100 each, you'll pocket a gain when Government does redeem. This may or may not be free of capital gains tax. It's the *return*—of *value*—that matters. Where there's a choice, which investment is likely to produce for you the best return—by when? That's the key question you have to find the answer to. It means weighing and comparing various risks: and just to make things more difficult, taking into account any taxation you may be liable for on interest or gain or both in each case, sooner or later.

4 At this point I'm going to jump ahead for the moment. It could help you to understand better if we had a look at the other side's point of view. There are, after all, two sides to any investment—the investor's and the investee's; the people who invest and those who are invested in. (If you invest in your own business, you're both, of course; but what we're talking about is investing in other people.) It's most important, by the way, to remember *always* that when you buy securities you're really investing in other people, because it's people—not things—that keep bargains—or don't. All securities are simply written evidence of bargains. That is to say, they're proofs of promises, and the problem with any promise is simply whether it will be kept or not; or how far it will be kept.

Mind you, there's often a third side as well, that of the broker or 'intermediary' who brings investors and investees together, gives advice, makes the deals, and charges for it.

Obviously, whether an intermediary's advice is good or bad is most important. There are many kinds of securities you can't buy except through an intermediary, anyway. People on the whole are apt to be far too careless about 'intermediaries'. You can't be too careful, but we'll come back to that later.

Suppose you wanted £10,000 to start a business. You don't know anyone likely to lend you so much. Short of pinching it, marrying it or winning it, there are only two ways of 'raising' it: by borrowing it from Tom, Dick and Harry, or by persuading them to 'buy rights' to a say in your business and a share of the profits you hope to make—i.e. buy shares of one kind or another in your enterprise.

Let's take borrowing first. You offer 'loan stock' in 'units' —dollops—of, say, £100: 100 units equals £10,000. You offer so much per cent interest a year and repayment ('redemption') of the face-value in so many years' time (five, ten, fifteen or what-have-you—or *when you feel like it*). To get Tom, Dick and Harry and others to buy your units, you'll have to offer 'terms' as good as other people are offering: better if they're thought 'safer', that's to say likelier to keep their promise than you. Will you be able to go on paying the promised interest? Will you be able to 'redeem' (buy back) your IOUs (pay the face-value) when due day comes?

Down the years—for centuries—one government after another has issued scores of different sorts of loan stocks at different rates of interest, redeemable in X, Y or Z years' time, or when Government feels like it: what are called 'dated' or 'undated' stocks. The face-value of all these stocks added together is prodigious: the *value*, of course, at any time, is another matter. They leak (or gain) value as fast as money does. They're bound to. They're merely a kind of money.

Much of the same applies to loan stocks (commonly called 'debentures' or 'preference shares') issued by industrial and commercial concerns. Here, of course, face-value can't be guaranteed because only Government can make money and tax value out of people to pay its debts with. In the case of commercial or industrial stocks, the promise is only as good as the promiser, who may look sounder than he (or it) really is. (Remember again Rolls-Royce!) Often they're 'secured': that is to say, if the business goes bankrupt, holders of secured stocks come at the head of the queue for a share of what the assets can be sold for. Sometimes they're 'unsecured', which means their holders don't. And sometimes they're 'convertible', which means that holders can swap them for ordinary shares (often called equities) in due course if they want to, which may prove well worth while if the enterprise does well. *If.*

If dividends from this or that business *look like* being bigger than they have been recently, the price of its ordinary shares will tend to go up in the (stock) market—and *vice versa.* So if you buy shares in it at the right time, you stand to gain in two ways—through growing dividends and profit if you sell the shares while their market price is higher than you've paid. However, if you buy them at the wrong time. . . . Ordinary shares, remember, have no face-value; they're not 'redeemable'. And since the return (yield plus profit) is in money, you must allow for value-leakage when you're trying to work out whether buying this or that kind is likely to bring you more (or less) value—some day—after allowing for tax on dividends and capital gains. Then ask yourself, 'How much *could* I gain? How much *could* I lose? Is the possible prize worth the risk?'

One thing for certain about ordinary shares. They're no kind of tools to hit investment *targets* with. No kind at all.

5 Now let's slip back to those medium-long and long-term targets—ten years or more away.

Coach-rides. . . . Funds, that's to say: funds being kitties lots of people pool their spare cash in with an eye to joint investing—sharing risks, gains and losses between them; leaving the problems of choosing and watching and switching investments to professional managers.

A fund, then, starts by being a 'stock' of money. As this money gets invested, it becomes a stock of properties. These properties may all be one kind—shares or land or land-and-buildings or loan stocks or 'commodities' such as metals or tea or cocoa or rubber or wool or raw cotton or any other kind of 'raw material'. Or gems or works of art or money itself or a mixture of some or all suitable kinds of property—suitable being any kind of property you can test for quality and quantity (more or less) and sell fairly easily. At least, that's the idea. Or should be.

Let's go back to that £10,000 you proposed to borrow in £100 loan stock units from Tom, Dick, Harry, Uncle Tom Cobbleigh and all, to start a business with. Instead of loan stock, you might of course offer shares at £1, say, apiece. What sort of business? they'd want to know. 'I'm very good at investing,' you might say. 'I propose to use our stock of money to buy a choice collection of ordinary shares with. If those shares do well—if those enterprises make tidy profits—our company will get good dividends from them, and profits from buying and selling the shares. You lot will get good dividends out of *our* dividends and profits and *our* shares will go up in price in the "market", and you'll make profits in your turn when you sell them.'

You'll have set up what is called an 'Investment Trust'.

There are a score or so good investment trusts * operating in Britain, and ordinary shares in them can be a good thing to hold.

A fund manager is primarily an investor—chasing value. Value, as you know, is a fickle thing, now here, now there—as the fitful winds of popular hope and fear blow this way or that. Consequently, the more widely a fund spreads its investments and the more easily and quickly it can change them by selling this and buying that, the better placed it is to catch and hold value—here, there or somewhere. Value flits from property to property, so it's safer to hold a variety of shares than shares of only one kind, a variety of commodities, a variety of buildings, a variety of any particular *kind* of investment. Value is also apt to flit from one *kind* of investment to another—from 'equities' (ordinary shares) to loan stocks, to land and buildings, to gems, to works of art, to equities, as the whims and moods of investors veer and blow.

A man of means who wants to stay a man of means will maintain a mixed bag of properties—of investments: what's called a 'balanced portfolio'. It's the same with a fund. If you aim to reach a target of value in ten or more years' time by investing in a fund, you must choose one that isn't liable to be full of value one day (or year) and three parts empty the next. You want one which can be relied upon—as far as anything can be—to deliver the goods on the nail.

This is why an endowment-assurance 'policy' is by far the best investment tool for hitting a target bang on. When you take out an endowment-assurance policy, you buy from a 'life office' the right to draw from its fund an agreed sum of money on an agreed date in the future; plus, should you die before that date, the right to have this sum paid to your estate or named heir, which is, of course, very handy if you've got a family.

* They're not trusts, actually. They're really joint-stock companies.

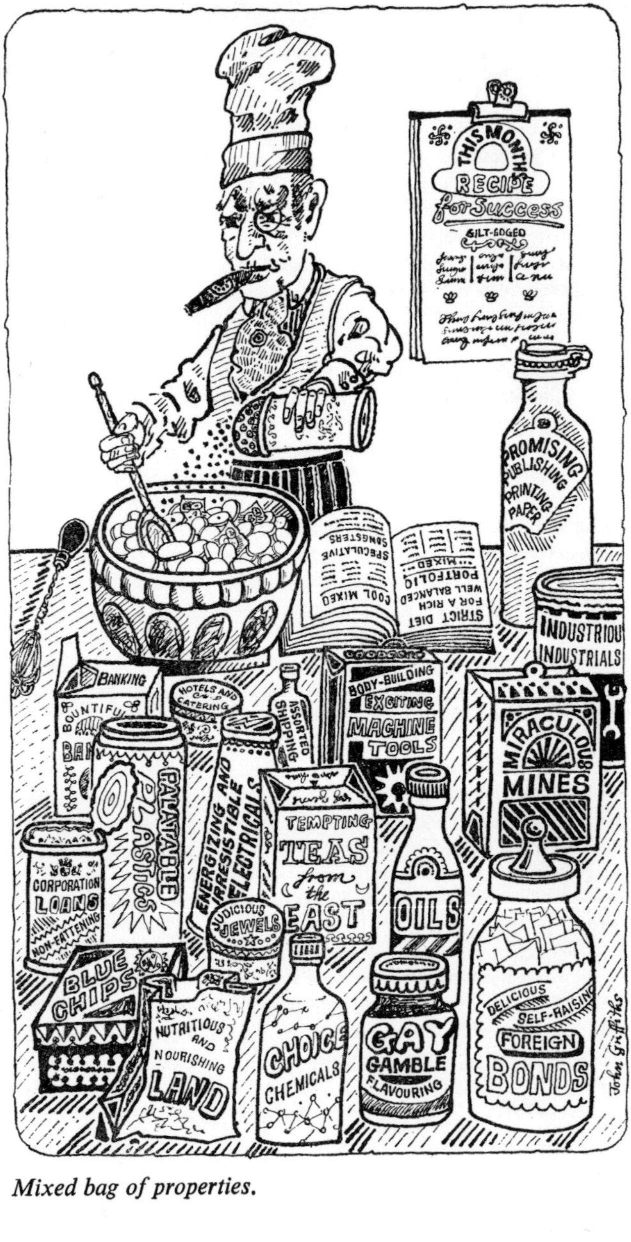

Mixed bag of properties.

The point is this: how life assurance actually works is horribly difficult to explain, so I won't try here. In a nutshell, though, 'offices' which run 'life funds' *guarantee* to pay their endowment policy-holders eventually more money from their funds than they'll have paid in. This they manage to do mainly by getting the extra money from investments bought with policy-holders' 'premiums' (contributions). This means they have to work out very carefully how much they're going to need to meet all claims in future and make sure they get that much—and more, to be on the safe side. This, in turn, means investing to get as much *yield* as possible without taking undue risks—i.e. by getting and keeping a very wide spread and mixture of investments. They go for fixed-interest yields from Government and other loan stocks, rents from land and factory, shop or office buildings, dividends from shares—the lot. In short, they make sure of getting back on the swings what they may lose on the roundabouts.

What's more, by playing it well on the safe side, they tend to collect by degrees more value in their funds than their policy-holders are likely to claim in money as time goes by. From time to time each office tots up its 'surplus', as they call it, and ladles a part of it out in the form of a money 'bonus' (dividend, really) to its 'with-profit' policy-holders who contribute extra money for the privilege. There's no tax on the gain you get from an endowment policy: that's one more advantage. Another—very real—one is the income-tax relief allowed on the premiums. If you're at all liable for income-tax at the present standard rate of 39½p in the pound, this relief means you can charge 15½p out of every pound you spend on endowment assurance to your fellow taxpayers. Within limits—which are unlikely to bother you.

Now these things—income-tax relief and exemption from capital gains tax—are obviously a great help. Thanks to these, the guaranteed-plus-the-likely-bonus return plus the life cover make a good ten-to-fifteen-year British 'with-profit' endowment policy easily the *soundest* long-range investment you can make: the ideal foundation of your 'fortune'.

'Good', I said, and 'soundest'. You won't make a 'killing' from any endowment-assurance policy, but that's not the point. The proper job of a foundation is to be 'sound'. As for 'good', well, there are scores of different 'offices' in Britain offering as many—and more—widely different recipes in different funds at widely different 'premium rates' (prices).

To find what's best or just good for you, you'll have to go picking and choosing.

6 There are drawbacks, naturally, to the ordinary endowment policy. As my old nanny used to say, 'You get nothing for nothing in this world.' You can't just get your money back out of a life fund when you feel like it. You can get a bit of it after a year or two. But the lot? Not for several. And that's *money*—not value. To get the full *value*, you must almost certainly stay the full course. Almost certainly? Well, nothing can be dead sure. A rich, well-invested British life fund is built to catch and hold value in any economic 'weather'. Still, anything *can* happen. And it takes time, anyway, for value to pile up in a life fund and find its way out to policy-holders. You can be unlucky over bonuses. Your policy may run through lean years.

As value leaks out of money, it's bound to go somewhere. The surest places are works of art, curios, gems: which is the main reason why our old miser friend collected such things (the other was vanity). There are snags, of course. It's very hard, for instance, to get any 'yield'—that's to say, income—out of such properties. And most people need income from their investments. Income plus, in due course, profit: the more (of both) the merrier—naturally.

Shares can produce both. So can loan stocks and some bonds. So can land and buildings, commonly called 'Property'. So can 'rights' of one sort or another such as copyrights, patents and concessions. In the case of loan stocks and bonds, both yields and profits are limited by fixed interest rates and face-values. With the others the sky's the limit—in theory anyway.

There's bound to be a limit—somewhere—somewhen—to the amount of value any property can attract. Nothing, after all, lasts for ever. The eternal questions are, of course—where? And when?

Now life offices *guarantee* to pay pre-agreed sums of *money*—that is to say, of face-value. These sums are targets—many of them far away in the future; and sound fixed-interest—fixed-*return*—securities are just the tools for the job. To fatten the surpluses they pay bonuses out of, however, they must collect *value*, so they also go in for shares, land and buildings in a big way. It's the hope of bigger and better bonuses which brings in the buyers of 'with-profit' endowment policies.

Naturally: because people like you and me don't often have to hit *face-value* targets far away in the future; what we need is supplies of *value*—enough at least to replace as time goes by what's for ever leaking out of the money we earn; and more if one wants to get better off, not merely stand still.

So we too could do with shares, land and buildings, commodities—(if not copyrights, patents and concessions)—gems, curios, works of art, anything likely to hold value better than money. The problem is how to pick and choose and buy and, for that matter, sell. Each includes a huge variety of different categories, types and specimens calling for a vast range of specialist knowledge. You can buy stocks and shares in quite small parcels through the highly organized market-places called Stock Exchanges. There's no such market, though (bar local auctions), for land and buildings, 'lots' of which tend to be big 'parcels' which call for big sums of money. There are commodity auction markets, but here too 'lots' are big and costly. Copyrights, concessions and the like are not for the small average investor. As for works of art, curios, gems, antiques, and so on—well, there are sale-rooms (auction-marts) as well as all the local shops and stalls where you can pick up the odd bargain if you know a thing or two—if, that's to say, you're a bit of an expert in some line yourself, or have one with you. Without the *right* special knowledge at your elbow you might just as well take your pick—which is gambling, not investing. You're gambling, remember, when you're obviously likelier to lose value through a buy than gain it: investing's the other way round.

There's far more money about now than ever before leaking value faster and faster, which means that far more ordinary people than ever before are looking for kinds of property likelier to hold, and preferably gain, value. Our splendid rambling old investment system largely built by the 'Forsytes' for the 'Forsytes' was not designed to cater for Everyman. However, if rambling, it's also adaptable. Bright boys in the money game long since sensed a widespread hankering, as it were, for 'choice assortments' of particular kinds of properties in popular sizes, and keep coming up with ingenious schemes to satisfy it. Much the best known of these schemes so far are the 'Unit Trusts'* associated with ordinary shares.

Units. Popular-size packets, so to speak, of assorted

* These are trusts, i.e. their assets are held by trustees.

'properties'. Particular kinds of. Like, say, sweets: assorted shapes, sizes, colours, flavours of—chocolates *or* fruit gums *or* candies *or* what-else. Or, indeed, of mixed *kinds*.

Already the huge range of assortments is bewildering, and few experts even seriously pretend to know offhand what's inside every packet—behind every enticing label. What they do know, though, is how to test assortments: how to analyse them and weigh the different kinds and degrees of risks. They're all more or less risky. They're bound to be.

7 More or less risky. More risky, for instance, than any decent with-profit endowment-assurance. Less risky than any *particular* stock—share—plot of land—building 'lot'—or anything else, you could invest in. That's the idea, anyway. I said 'choice assortment'. What amateur investors need is not just handy sizes but a ready-made 'mixed portfolio' in miniature. Assortment spreads risks, but it takes knowledge and skill to choose and collect a likely assortment—and keep it likely.

What happens? In principle, anyway? You and others pay money to a unit trust. The Managers use this money to buy various ordinary shares—less their rake-off for running the business. They collect their 'choice portfolio' (assortment). For your money, you and other subscribers get credited with so many 'units', i.e. standard, handy-sized particles of the 'portfolio's' cash-value. The price of each share in the portfolio goes up and down on the London Stock Exchange, so the cash-value of the whole portfolio varies from day to day. Each of your units is a right to a particle of the portfolio's cash-value, so its cash-value likewise varies in line with the portfolio's.

The prices of some shares go up each day while others go down or stay put. So the cash value of one assortment can increase while another's decreases. So the price any unit trust charges for its units and will pay to buy units back likewise tends to vary, and this will differ from trust to trust. If, then, you collect the units of a particular trust by paying in a fixed sum every so often—every month, say—over several years, you'll average out the cost of your collection, getting more units when prices are low than when they're high. You'll make no 'killing' this way: but then unit trusts are not there for unit holders to make 'killings' from. 'Killings' are for venturers, promoters, and people in the know or able to put two and two together.

Unit trust managers buying shares

So you can buy units in batches occasionally or regularly and sell all or some of them back when it suits you; or you can buy different 'brands' if you want (or can afford) to: make a mixed 'portfolio' of them, in fact. If, however, you go in for a regular-subscription-for-ten-years-or-more package with a dash of life cover in it (called 'unit-linked assurance') you can qualify for the sizable advantage of that 15½p in the pound subsidy from income-tax relief conceded to ordinary endowment-assurance. That ten-years-or-more, by the way, applies also to ordinary endowments: in either case, if you don't stay the course, you jeopardize the income-tax reliefs. Incidentally you may run into capital gains tax on profits made out of unit collections.

What you own if you buy a unit of this kind is, as I said, the right to have a particle—a fraction—of the cash-value of a collection of ordinary shares. Why stop at shares? What about other classes of properties—land, bricks and mortar, loan stocks, commodities, gems, works of art, etc.? Why not make collections of these and sell unit claims ditto on their cash-values? The answer is—people do. 'Property Bonds' (units of commercial land and buildings portfolios) have been selling like nobody's business for the last year or two. 'Commodity' units are offered and so are units of farmland and buildings. Some years back an attempt was made to market units of collections of diamonds. You could do it in theory with pictures — silver — antiques — curios — copyrights. *In theory*. . . .

In practice? Well, if you're honestly selling fractions of future cash-value which buyers may claim from you at any time, the first thing you must be able to do is measure the cash-value of your collection of properties accurately at any time. Secondly, you must have cash handy to give to claimants should large numbers of them—somewhat suddenly—want to sell their units back to you.

This cash, *in theory*, you can always raise by selling (realizing) items of your collection. However, it's not quite as simple as that. How do you find the buyers—quickly? How much will they be likely to pay when it comes to the toss for this item or that?

With stocks and shares, it's relatively easy. There are those highly organized 'market-places', the Stock Exchanges, which vet the enterprises whose shares they allow to be 'quoted', i.e. offered for sale on their 'floors'. Prices paid for all 'quoted' securities are recorded daily, so if you own a collection, you can easily value (get a cash price for) each item every day. You can also—*as a rule*—sell items easily to raise cash. It's obviously far more difficult to determine from day to day or even from year to year the market-value of particular parcels of land or buildings: nor can you often sell any of them quickly to raise cash. There are highly organized auction markets for commodities, true; but the prices of commodities are notoriously frisky. The prices of gems are infinitely less switchback, less risky (as long as they're good) but the cash-value of any collection or item is pretty well a matter of guesswork till it's sold. As for art collections—well, the value of any work of art is what it will fetch, and it takes a well-publicized auction sale to get the best price.

So, you see, there are some real practical difficulties, some wonderful opportunities for artful charlies, and some awful lurking perils for artless investors in this game.

As long as you realize that when you buy units in any kind of collection, you're investing not in the collection but in its future cash-value, which may be anything. Quite a few trusts, by the way, sell units of the yield and of the capital value separately: holders of one kind share the future income from the portfolio; holders of the other, the gain (if any) in its future cash-value.

You're buying, with every unit, the right to be paid a bit of the cash-value, on the day you demand it, of the collection named by the unit-sellers. *This need not be theirs*. It often isn't. It may simply be an 'index'—an assortment dreamed up by others. In theory, one could sell 'units' of the cash-value on any given day of the pictures in the Tate Gallery—the Beaulieu vintage cars collection—the treasures in the British Museum—or any other 'gold mine'. When tempted, therefore, wonder and ask: What's the recipe? What kinds of property or properties? What particular items? Who tots up the cash-value of this collection? How do they do it? Who checks the figures? How often? Will They have the cash to pay me and others when we want it? How? Who are They, anyway? What will the collection consist of in two—five—ten or more years' time? Will it contain quite different items? If so, how can anyone even begin to gauge *now* what its cash-value is *likely* to be *then*? . . . And what's *their* rake-off? And what becomes of the *income*?

If you think about it, you'll realize that when you buy shares and units, what you're really investing in is the skill and foresight and honesty of people—directors and managers. Skilful people aren't necessarily honest; honest people aren't necessarily skilful; and neither necessarily have foresight. *And they change as time goes by.*

Perhaps I should add that Her Majesty's Department of Trade and Industry can do and does a good deal to hamper and discourage artful charlies from taking you one way or another for too much of a ride. In the end, though, only you can really protect yourself, by taking a long, cool look at all invitations to join band-wagons, and by invariably declining them when in doubt. Treat *all* ads and salesmen as 'guilty' till *proved* 'innocent' by expert *independent* witness.

Needless to say, there are numerous unit band-wagons—the better life offices among them—whose integrity and solidity you can rely on, so far as you can rely on anything in times of frantic change like these.

8 'Nothing venture,' mind you, 'nothing have,' to quote dear old nanny again.

The time to take to venturing is *after* you've provided for your money targets, needless to say. As good an investment as you can make, by the way, is a *good* house of your own. By 'good', I mean one that should still be as 'desirable' a 'residence': in ten years' time—all things considered. If you buy one with a mortgage loan, it can pay you to arrange repayment of the loan by a 'matching' endowment-assurance because of the income-tax allowances for premiums and loan interest. Repaying a mortgage loan is the commonest of all major targets, I'd suppose: non-profit endowment is the tool for such long-term 'debt redemption', as they call it. You pay extra for a 'with-profit' policy, and if you've reached the 'venture-stage' it's worth your while to have a go at something livelier with that extra. Units, for instance. Units are a good introduction to 'equities', apart from their particular merits.

They're not the same thing, as you'll have realized, I hope. An equity unit (I'll repeat) gives you a right to a fraction of the cash-value of—or yield from—an assortment of ordinary shares. An ordinary share gives the right to a bit of as much of the net annual profit of a business as the directors see fit to distribute to shareholders; and of what's left if the business fails after all other debts have been paid. Read that again—slowly. It means that you can't count on getting fat dividends even from fat profits. There can be a lot of 'undistributed' value lurking in the assets of a business, which often gets 'released' if it's taken over. But if a business goes bankrupt, its ordinary shares often become mere waste paper.

What this means is that the market price of a share doesn't necessarily reflect the value of assets (properties) of one kind and another lurking *behind* it. The market price of a share is partly set by the 'yield' boffin people reckon to get from it *in due course*, partly by what return shrewd people reckon other (less shrewd) people will hope to get from it in due course, and partly by what many people just hope and believe. Read that one again, too—slowly. Three winds blow value into and out of shares: 'calculation', 'flair' and 'sentiment'—what some people reckon, some foresee and many just hope for. Investors—speculators—gamblers.

People say you might as well pick shares with a pin as use your wits for the job. This is only true if you're trying to make quick profits—'playing the market'. The people who do this are either gamblers or speculators. Investors usually stay out of excited markets. Prices, they know, are yo-yos. If the value's there or coming—or not there or going—well, it's bound to get spotted and shift the price eventually one way or the other. Patience, they know well, is *the* virtue.

They know, you see, that value is something generated in a property—or kind of it—by the pressure of the 'wind' of human demand, which is apt to be fitful and blustery, and to veer wildly. They don't chase the wind as most amateurs do. They watch the weather, so to speak, try to forecast which way it's likely to blow before long, then search out and buy the particular properties likeliest to generate the most value when the wind does blow that way. They steal aside on their own, you might say, while the others are all flocking in one direction, take their pick—and wait. Sometimes they shout, 'Hey! Look, everybody, what I've found', to attract attention when they're ready. Sometimes they'll prompt others to flock in the opposite direction first. There's an old story of Baron Rothschild getting the news of Waterloo by pigeon before anyone else, and walking across the Stock Exchange 'floor' looking very glum. As he had a great reputation for being in the know, people guessed Napoleon must have won, and rushed to sell stocks. Value evaporated . . . prices sank like stones. Secretly, Rothschild bought stocks 'for a song'. Then came the real news—and prices soared again as the

In the know . . .

panickers thronged back to buy. Rothschild made a 'killing'. Yes, you need a big reputation to pull off that sort of coup. However, since people are always trying to do so, let it serve as a warning to you never to act on a Stock Market tip. Ninety-nine times out of a hundred such tips are bait for mugs.

Can you—an 'amateur'—invest in shares without being a mug? The short answer is—Yes, but not always. Not even experts can do that. Nobody, you see, can know everything. Everyone has to take some things on trust, i.e. at face-value, and that's the camouflage over the traps. What you can do, though, is side-step enough of the traps to stand a fair chance of doing well—even very well.

The first rule is to find, get and stick to a good and honest adviser. Before you do this, though, there's quite a bit you can—and should—do for yourself. Map out your 'quest'. Like this, for instance:

1 Pick one or two really big *looming* national (or global) problems; pollution, say, or traffic: or leisure: or population explosion. Study them a bit (consult your local librarian and read the 'quality' papers, especially the serious weekly reviews). In short take an interest in tomorrow's world.

2 Search out the names of firms likely to tackle the problems you pick in some way or other. These you can spot in the relevant trade publications. (Again, consult your local librarian.) What aspects of, say, the growing pollution problem look the most pressing and likeliest to be tackled first on the biggest scale? Which of the *smaller, less known, but livelier go-ahead* enterprises look as if they might grab the opportunites and prosper—and *grow*?

3 Make a game of it—a hobby. It can be as fascinating as any, and, with some luck and plenty of horse-sense, profitable—even very profitable—as well.

4 Look for and keep looking for the livelier enterprises—those, that's to say, with the livelier managements. But don't (unless you can't help yourself) go further than this. *Don't* try to take enterprises to pieces, so to speak, yourself, to see how they tick and what they consist of. This is a job which calls for special knowledge, special know-how and special tools. This is the job for that good and honest adviser. He's crucial. What and where is he?

Well, the short answer to that is that he's an authorized stockbroker—member of a Stock Exchange. You could write to the London Stock Exchange for information and advice; there's certainly no harm in that. Or to the City page editor of a major newspaper. You should remember, though, that it doesn't at present pay the average stockbroking firm to handle 'small' deals—deals for less than £500- to £1,000-worth of shares at a time. So your best plan to start with is probably to go to your bank manager (once you've got a bank account, needless to say). Tell him what field and firms you're interested in and ask him to get advice from the stockbroking firm he deals through on behalf of customers like you. This is one of the many useful services the clearing banks provide.

Buy shares for medium term—two to five years'—growth. Don't try to 'play the market' for quick profits. You stand a poor chance of winning unless you're on the spot—'on the floor' of the Exchange—yourself or have an expert there to seize the passing chances for you. Don't be greedy: take a decent profit if your adviser thinks you should. And (what's far more difficult) don't be proud: cut losses if your adviser thinks you should: sell and try something else. And remember advisers are human. They too can make mistakes, or be deceived—or tempted.

In the end, it all comes back to people. It's the adviser who matters. If you can pick (and interest) good advisers, you can pick anything. 'And interest'? Well, if you evidently know a fair bit about, say, the anti-pollution business, you might be able to tell *him* quite a bit. As I said, nobody can possibly know everything or, for that matter, ever enough.

You could boil it all down to this, really: and it applies to every—yes, *every*—field of investment: stocks—shares—property—works of art—gems—commodities—anything which could attract *value.* Go for what's good but *out of fashion.* Try to foresee by study what sort of things could or should become fashionable—i.e. in demand—in a few years' time. Get a good and honest *practical* expert to advise you on what *is* good in each field and, if possible, to make the deals for you.

And never forget it's value you're after—not the face-value of money: value *after* you've allowed for leakage *and taxation* of the return—of the yield (if any) and of the profit: both: separately and put together. Income-tax and capital gains tax.

9 And here, I suppose, I'd better stop. One could go on all night into details—the pros and cons of this or that: for ever, to be sure. The details are endlessly changing. That's the trouble. Investing is a quest for value—endless because value is for ever restless. Where—in what properties or kinds of property—is it likely to collect next? And multiply? Or linger —for how long?

Everybody, nearly, is chasing value. Most chase it in money which should but can't hold it. Those who already have a lot of it, keep, if they're wise, many different kinds of property for it to nestle in. Laws guard the right of ownership. Those who own a lot, or aim to, seek to preserve the laws which guard their rights. Those who have little seek to change the laws to their own advantage. Mostly they achieve this (or think they do) through taxation—now of this, now of that sort of property: now in this way, now in that. Value flits from the sorts which are most to the ones that are least taxed or where there are handy legal loopholes for avoidance.

These are revolutionary times. If one thing's certain it is that nothing's certain. You can't safely count on present investment conditions staying the same for more than a year or two—if that. Where will value crop up—or down— when Britain is in the Common Market—or isn't for that matter?

So, to invest well and to be well invested, you must above all be footloose—alert—well advised—and nimble.

And shrewd.

It's easy enough to be well advised, on paper anyway, if you're rich already. You just hire the advisers with the big reputations—the ones in the know—and, if you're as suspicious as our old miser, play them off against each other. Mind you, he got milked far more than he supposed (he loved to think he was as shrewd as the devil) but he could afford it, and, in any case, he could only judge things—and people—by their price, so being milked by advisers was, you might say, in a sense a pleasure. The world's top skills, he loved to think, were his toys, his puppets.

If you aren't rich, you have to be really shrewd, that's to say worldly—knowing! Knowing about people as individuals and as mobs, the way they tend to behave. This was where 'Old Blubberguts' scored. He'd come up the hard way using his wits and learning all the time. There were no flies on Old B, whereas there'd always been plenty on the POM in the sense of his having long been, for all practical purposes—dead. Old B really was as shrewd as the devil, perhaps shrewder. Which takes me back to that crashed aircraft, and the question we left in the air. What was the most valuable property there in that situation? The big diamond—the six cans of beer—or something else altogether?

Let me go on with the story. The pilot and Old B were each thinking, if you remember, how enormously the other would be improved, as Saki put it, by death.

'The man's a fool,' Old B thought. 'Therefore. . . .' And the next time he had occasion to take a stroll, he quickly buried the diamond out of the pilot's sight, marked the spot and, returning to the aircraft, asked casually for a can of beer. 'You realize, by the way, my friend,' he said, 'that you could never dispose of the diamond, in case any such idea has crossed your mind? I took the precaution in London of leaving certain instructions with my lawyers—in case of accident, you understand. (As you know, I never omit precautions if I can help it.) Those instructions express certain misgivings and include the possibility of *your* surviving an accident—which was fatal to *me—without* the diamond, if you see what I mean. You would find it almost impossible, my lawyers reckoned, to explain *convincingly* to anyone *why* you hadn't the diamond. I won't bother to go into the details which would incriminate you, but I can assure you they would be—well—'damning' is what my lawyers called them. Discretion has never been your strong suit, my friend—or my wife's.'

These things and others he said with great guile, watching the pilot closely for give-away reactions as he played upon his impulsive nature. 'You see,' he said eventually, 'the diamond is now missing. If I died of thirst (or anything else) and you were rescued. . . . In no time. . . .' He gestured the rest.

The pilot, who was quite guileless, stared—dumbstruck. The possibility that Old B might be bluffing never occurred to him. Before it could, Old B was in there offering a deal, well worth grabbing, surely, in the circumstances? £25,000 for half the beer, and he'd finance any expedition the pilot cared to name.

The pilot fell for this, and three cans of beer went across to Old B. So the diamond proved not valueless after all—as long as it was 'lost' . . . an interesting thought. The most valuable property there, though, was surely the old so-and-so's shrewdness: his guile: his skill which played and landed the pilot?

As a matter of interest, they and the diamond were rescued in the nick of time. When it came to keeping his promises, Old B found endless excuses for not doing so. One day he was discovered battered to death in his house near Jo'burg. Three Bantu were arrested, tried and hanged. For reasons which amused but rather puzzled their acquaintances, the pilot stayed on with old B's widow as a secretary-cum-chauffeur for a while. She was a tough customer by any standard, and gossip liked to hint that the pair of them had to hang together, being unable to trust each other apart. It was even suggested uncharitably that the Bantu could have been put up to the job done on Old B.

The big diamond, by the way, went for a Burton. She sold it off. It reminded her—and others—of Old B.

Mind you, from time to time, she lavished presents on him of the gold cigarette-case and sapphire studs and cuff-links variety. He had to be a credit to her. After all, her poodles had mink jackets and collars studded with pearls and things.

A credit.

He took to drink.

Luckily, one night before long, in a Monte Carlo bar (she haunted all the jet-set tax-havens), he bumped into a party of wild-life documentary film-makers who were prospecting for a spot of financial backing and were in need of a congenial colleague who could handle a light aircraft. Among them was a girl with a passion for salvaging lame ducks or dogs and rescuing captive creatures from thraldom of any kind. Well, to cut a long story short, he sold all his precious gewgaws (Old B would have pledged the things to a bank for a loan, naturally: they were bound to gain value: one would be mad to part with them) and invested the cash proceeds in an expedition to film birds and animals and people in outlying Indonesia. In time, the films they made did well on television, and so did amusing books he wrote about this and subsequent excursions. And—yes—the girl married him. And they got much fun out of life. They still do. Which only goes to show something, I suppose: that wise people invest, for instance, to do their own thing—not somebody else's.

3 Test Yourself Questions

1 What investment targets would suit you? What periods would you set for them? [Section 1]

2 What are the main snags about 'contractual' money-saving plans? What arrangement gives you the most freedom for manœuvre? [Section 2]

3 What is the difference between a 'redeemable' and an 'irredeemable' stock? Why do loan stock prices vary from time to time? [Section 3]

4 Why are ordinary shares riskier than commercial loan stocks? [Section 4]

5 What is an investment trust? What is a 'mixed portfolio'? Why is a good British endowment-assurance the ideal foundation for a 'fortune'? [Section 5]

6 What is a 'unit'? If you own one what does it entitle you to? Why do unit prices go up and down? What should you 'wonder and ask' when tempted to invest in units of any kind? [Sections 6 and 7]

7 What 'makes' the market-price of a share? Why is market-price apt to be deceptive? What is the most important thing to get and have before you make an investment? [Section 8]

Postscript

'Don't try to think, boy,' an old teacher of mine used to growl. 'It's no good trying to think without the proper apparatus.' That goes for doing anything properly, and it means, among other things, knowing the theory before tackling the practice, walking before you take to running.

This little book is largely theory with general guides to practice. If you have really taken its messages in, you will possess the basic knowledge to guide you, to avoid blunders and to resist foolish temptations.

Beware of all advertisements and salesmen inviting you to invest. This doesn't mean ignore them. It means never take them at their face-value. Firms advertise and sell to do themselves more good than you—sometimes to do you no good at all. Commercial advertising is the art of prompting people to deceive themselves. People, you see, tend to believe what they want to read or hear: so all commercial ads blow up the likely benefits they offer and play down the snags where they don't leave them out altogether, hoping you won't notice them. They aim to tempt and dazzle, some a lot, some only a little. Naturally, it's the most tempting and dazzling you need to be wariest of.

It's the same with salesmen, only more so. A salesman, though, has far more scope for tempting you than any ad. If you must listen to a salesman, remember all the time you're listening that what he's after is his commission on a sale. Remember that every salesman who's any good is methodically and artfully trying to manœuvre you into a pen, much as a trained sheepdog manœuvres a sheep into a pen. What a good salesman does, though, is to tempt, tease and prod or goad you into building the pen yourself without your realizing it. This pen will largely consist of your own pride. He'll slyly get your agreement to a series of general propositions which you won't like to retreat from later, when he turns the heat on you, for fear of looking silly. He'll use all sorts of ploys and devices to make you feel stupid or mean or anything else contemptible if you don't do what he suggests. The important thing is to be thoroughly awkward all the time, asking yourself what *trustworthy independent* evidence is there that what he's offering is anything like as promising as he says or implies it is. Never—*never* sign anything at a first meeting, and *never—never—never* part with any money in any form whatever. Always insist on his leaving his proposition on paper with you for several days, and try to get the advice on it of a bank manager, a solicitor, an accountant or someone with real investment knowledge. Your local Citizens' Advice Bureau can often get you sound advice. Even then, if you get a green light, *always* insist on having the offer made to you in writing, signed preferably by someone responsible in the firm's office—at any rate, *signed in writing*. Salesmen don't always say only what their employers would prefer them to say and their memories can be shocking. When you do have the offer in writing, read it thoroughly and weigh its implications with great care—with expert *disinterested* advice, for preference—before you sign anything whatever yourself or part with a brass farthing or 1p piece.

Show, in short, that you could be interested but are clearly no fool. You're most unlikely to miss anything worth having, believe me, if you do this. What's more important, you're unlikely to lose something you would miss very much—a slice of your own hard-won value.

As time goes by, you will probably want to know more about different fields and kinds of investments. I hesitate to list books, of which there are dozens, simply because they tend to get out of date. As far as books are concerned, I think your best plan is to consult your nearest big library. What books have they on investment and which are the best and latest? Or what could they get for you? More important, really, is to keep an eye on the best weekly and monthly papers dealing with politics, economics, finance and investments. Again, your local library will advise you about these. When considering financial investment, write for advice to the City Editor of any of the national daily or Sunday newspapers. Newspapers side with their readers.

For general information, write also to any of the organizations whose addresses are given on p. 85, bearing in mind only that associations, trade or otherwise, exist to serve the interests of their members and are therefore most unlikely to give you any advice which could imply that one member is in any way better than or not as good as any other. Broadly speaking, trade associations can only tell you what facilities exist and how their businesses work. They can't much help you to choose. It's important to know broadly how things work, but it's far more important to know how to choose, and here, as I've said so many times, only *disinterested* expert advice can help you. Look for it—and make sure you know in advance how much, if anything, it's going to cost you.

And Before You Plunge . . .

There are quite a few questions you need *reliable* answers to. When you invest, remember, you *buy* something to get *value*—which means somebody *sells* something to you. His offer is 'a pig in a poke'. Do you take his word for it that the pig is a good pig or even a pig at all? Therefore, there are four key questions you must ask and keep asking yourself, since you are bound to have to take some things on trust.

1 Who says it's a good buy?
2 Why does he say so?
3 Does he actually know or is he just a repeater?
4 Why should I believe him?

There are two main kinds of other questions—some to do with arithmetic and others to do with people. The arithmetical ones concern (*a*) how much money you will be likely to get and keep as time goes by and (*b*) how much value you will be likely to get and keep as time goes by. Taking the arithmetical ones first. . . .

1 What yield (interest, dividends, rents, bonuses, etc.) can this investment provide? Is it fixed—so much a year?
2 How much tax might I have to pay on yield?
3 How much profit could buying and selling it produce?
4 How much tax might I have to pay on profit?
5 How often is yield paid and when?
6 How much will it cost me to invest and disinvest in it?
7 How much value is likely to leak out of money while I hold this investment? How far will the *net* (after expenses and tax) return make up for the leakage?
8 What risks are there?

If you deposit money with the Government, remember you can count on getting your face-value back but *not* value. No other organization can *guarantee* face-value back in future and no organization of any kind can *guarantee* to produce any amount of value in future. Value attaches to assets, tangible and/or intangible. Tangible assets are solid properties such as land, buildings, machines, vehicles, etc. Intangibles are powers, rights, privileges, concessions, connections, commercial reputation, technical and managerial skills.

The future success and value of any business depend on how well its Management uses its assets. No Management, though, can do any better than it's allowed to by the people who *control* the business—the Board of Directors or, often, a group of them owning a lot of the shares between them.

Businesses are tools for getting value in money for shareholders; how much they get depends entirely on how they are run by Top Management—that's to say the Controlling Interests. Before you buy and as long as you hold stocks, shares or units of any business, therefore, you need to know:

1 What is its Top Management after? Expanding the business? A quiet life? Milking value from its assets?
2 What assets, tangible and intangible, does the business own? At what prices are they valued in the balance sheet? Might they fetch more if sold off? Or less?

The market-price of a share, you see, *should* reflect (*a*) the future dividends the business might pay and (*b*) the price its assets would fetch if sold off. It often doesn't. Why? Because it's commonly very difficult to find reliable answers to those questions.

It's the job of businesses which invest the money of unitholders and policyholders in ordinary shares etc. to find answers as far as they can, but you need to ask the same basic questions—and others—about *Them.*

1 Who are They? What is Their reputation?
2 How experienced are They? ('Whizz-kids', like rockets, are apt to plummet as well as soar.)
3 What is Their rake-off? How much would They charge for 'expenses of management'?

And after that, there are other questions:

4 What properties does the portfolio consist of *now*?
5 Will it change as time goes by?
6 What happens to the yield from the properties in the portfolio?
7 Is there a guaranteed minimum cash benefit? If so, how much?
8 Will I have to accept the cash price of the units on the date

of maturity even if it's low, or could I keep them till the price is better?

9 Could I rely on getting cash from Them for my units if there was a rush of holders wanting to sell them back some day? In other words, would They have enough cash handy (if so, how?) or could They easily sell their trust's holdings in order to get it?

10 Those first eight questions.

Needless to say, there's really no end to the questions you could ask. But they all come back to this in the end. . . .

When you invest in a Business you invest in its Management. Today's—and tomorrow's. Watch it.

List of Addresses

Association of Insurance Brokers	112 Kingsway London WC2
Association of Unit Trust Managers	Secretary 306 Salisbury House Finsbury Circus London EC2
Banking Information Service	10 Lombard Street London EC3
Building Societies Association	14 Park Street London W1
Corporation of Insurance Brokers	15 St Helens Place London EC3
The Life Offices' Association and Associated Scottish Life Offices	Aldermary House Queen Street London EC4N 1TP and 23 St Andrew Square Edinburgh 2
National Savings Committee	Alexandra House Kingsway WC2B 6TS
The Stock Exchange	Public Relations Officer London EC2
Trustee Savings Banks Association	Knighton House 52–66 Mortimer Street London W1

Some More Books to Read

Investment

CUMMINGS, Gordon. *The Complete Guide to Investment.* 5th ed. London, Penguin, 1970. 240 pp.

GWINNER, Christopher. *A Plain Guide to Investment.* London, Constable, 1969. 240 pp.

ROWLATT, James, and DAVENPORT, David. *Guide to Saving and Investment.* Revised ed. London, Pan Books, 1970. 260 pp.

Public Relations

BOWMAN, Pat, and ELLIS, Nigel. *Manual of Public Relations*; foreword by Herbert Lloyd and John Dodge. London, Heinemann, 1969. 287 pp.

JEFKINS, Frank William. *Advertising Today.* London, Intertext, 1971.

LLOYD, Herbert. *Teach Yourself Public Relations.* 2nd ed. London, Teach Yourself Books, 1971.

Index